Shari McMillan, Marquette Heights, Illinois, hand pieced this quilt named Shari's Baskets with black and red cotton sateen and hand quilted it using black thread. Shari had seen a similar quilt and in the process of trying to duplicate it, created her own pattern.

BASKETS OF TREASURES

BY
E DIE MCGINNIS

KANSAS CITY STAR BOOKS

ACKNOWLEDGEMENTS

I want to thank the Hawley family of the Arabia Steamboat Museum for letting me tell their story and for allowing us to take photos.

I would like to express my appreciation to Jan and Doug Bratcher of Bratcher Cooperage, 109 S. Water, Liberty, Missouri, 64068 - (816) 781-3988 - for lending us some wonderful barrels and kegs to use as props when photographing the quilts.

Thanks to the ladies who tested my patterns: Susie Kepley, Jane Miller, Mary Andrews, Bami Drinkwater, Jan Keeler, Dee Clevenger, Clara Diaz, Alta Short, Rosemary Garten, Margaret Falen, Shari McMillan, Peggy and Corky Hutinett, Linda Kriesel, Ruby Short, Brenda Butcher and Karlene Cooper. Karlene not only tested a pattern but opened her home to all of us rowdy quilters so we could get the quilt sewn together for this book.

Thanks to Rita Briner of Quilter's Station, Lee's Summit, Missouri, for being my sounding board and for pushing me out of my comfort zone.

Thanks to Vicky Frenkel for her lovely page design and great imagination and to Bill Krzyzanowski for adding to this book with his great photography skills. I also want to thank Judy Pearlstein for adding her special touch with her copy editing skills.

I also want to thank the people who have shared their quilts with us: Judy Streu, Liberty, Missouri; Shari McMillan, Marquette Heights, Illinois; Janette Luehring, Prairie Village, Kansas; Elizabeth Smith, Grandview, Missouri; and Judy Hill, Independence, Missouri.

Baskets of Treasures

By Edie McGinnis

Copy Editor: Judy Pearlstein
Designer: Vicky Frenkel
Photography: Bill Krzyzanowski

Published by Kansas City Star Books.

First edition.

ISBN: 0-9746012-3-3

Printed in the United States of America by Walsworth Publishing Co., Marceline, Missouri

To order copies, call StarInfo at (816) 234-4636 and say "BOOKS."

Order on-line at www.TheKansasCityStore.com.

TABLE OF CONTENTS

The Steamboat Arabia strikes a submerged snag south of Parkville, Missouri. Painting courtesy of Arabia Steamboat Museum.

INTRODUCTION

When I was a child of seven or eight, I carried most of my treasures around in my pockets: jacks, a buckeye, my skate key, pennies or nickels and whatever else might grab my attention at the moment.

David Hawley of Independence, Missouri, was far more ambitious when it came to treasure. He found a treasure map behind an abandoned miner's cabin while vacationing in Colorado with his family. He was eight years old. The hand-drawn map had been stuffed into a tin can.

This quilt book is dedicated to the adventurer in all of us. Whenever you feel like expanding your horizons, step out, take a chance, dig down and find the treasure of creativity that we somehow stuff away as we grow up. Before we start quilting though, let's get back to our story.

David and his family returned to Colorado for several years running, checking out court records and looking for gold. They didn't find anything but it wasn't for lack of trying. In any case, the entire family had been attacked by the treasure-hunting bug.

As adults, David and his brother, Greg, worked for their father, Bob, who owned a refrigeration business in Independence, Missouri. While out on a service call, David was chatting with his customer and noticed a map of the Missouri River hanging on the gentleman's wall. The map showed places where steamboats had sunk.

The family met at a local restaurant with their friend Jerry Mackey and discussed the possibility that the map might just lead them to realize their dream of finding buried treasure. After spending years studying old records and papers at the library and tromping through muddy creek beds, the Hawleys ended up with a large notebook full of information. They first narrowed the field of boats to ten. Upon more investigation, they settled on one.

The Hawleys and businessmen Jerry Mackey and David Luttrell formed River Salvage Inc. The company set out to find the remains of a steamboat named The Arabia, which had sunk south of Parkville, Missouri, in 1856.

The boat had caught a snag, a walnut tree hidden beneath the river's surface. Within hours most of the boat, with its hold laden with over 200 tons of cargo, had disappeared from view. The upper cabins of the boat remained above the water level enabling the passengers and crew to escape. Only one life was lost, that of a mule that had been tied to a piece of machinery and forgotten in the confusion.

Gone were the passengers' belongings and the precious cargo, not the least of which was 400 barrels of fine Kentucky bourbon whiskey. The few possessions the passengers managed to rescue were looted on the banks of the river while the victims searched for a place to stay the night and rest. Within three days the boat had disappeared completely.

In 1877, 1897 and 1974, attempts were made to recover the cargo of the Arabia. All were unsuccessful until River Salvage Inc. came on the scene in 1987. Using a metal detector and relying on old river maps to find the final resting place of the steamboat, David Hawley discovered the wreck lying underground in a field belonging to Norman and Beulah Sortor. With permission from the Sortors, the salvage company began digging 18 months later, after rounding up labor, money and machinery.

The excavation began after Bob Hawley determined how to keep water out of the hole. They installed 20 wells that could pump water at a rate of 1,000 cubic feet per minute. With the help of backhoes and heavy construction equipment, owned by David Luttrell, the dig was on.

After making a hole about the length of a football field and forty feet down, the partners found their first glimpse of treasure. It was a barrel of dishes covered in muck and mud. They stood hip deep in the mire and pulled 178 dishes out of the barrel.

There was more to come - a lot more. There were hats, boots, shoes, thimbles, china, tools, cigars, jewelry, pie filling, pickles, perfume, calico and silk. That was just the beginning. Preserving the shoes and boots alone could keep someone busy for years.

So what does a salvage company do with over 200 tons of artifacts dug from a field? It could have sold the treasure in order to recoup the cost of the adventure. Instead, the partners presented this generation and those who will follow a most magnificent museum. It is a history lesson on what life was like for those living over one hundred years ago.

If you have a trip to Kansas City in mind, don't miss the opportunity to see this marvelous collection.

The Arabia Steamboat Museum is open from 10 a.m. to 5:30 p.m. Monday through Saturday and from noon to 5 p.m. on Sunday. You will find the museum in the River Market area of Kansas City at Fourth Street and Grand Avenue. The last tour begins 90 minutes before closing time. Call 816-471-4030 for information or go to www.1856.com on the internet.

There are all kinds of treasure in the Kansas City area. One was the legacy left to the quilters by *The Kansas City Star*. In the archives are those great patterns designed by McKim, Foland and Dunn and sent in by readers of *The Star*. This book holds a treasure trove of basket patterns. Some are old, some are new but all will look wonderful in a quilt that is sure to be treasured by future generations.

Now come along and see what would have interested the ladies of 1856. I'm not so sure that it is all that different from what we quilters enjoy today. Okay, so maybe there were no rotary cutters but I think you can find plenty to treasure among the artifacts found on the steamboat. Perhaps one of the thimbles? Or maybe some buttons? Or maybe . . . well, you decide.

H o w T o

All of the patterns in this book are accompanied by templates. The templates are great for quilters who enjoy piecing by hand. They are also helpful when piecing on the machine, especially when the pieces are of an odd shape or measurement.

Just in case you might not want to use the templates, here are a few helpful hints for speeding up the piecing process.

Half Square Triangles

When making half square triangles, determine the finished size of the square needed. Add 7/8" to that measurement and cut accordingly. For example, if you want the half square triangle unit to be a 3" finished square, you would cut 3-7/8" squares. Place two squares together with the right sides facing each other and the edges aligned. Draw a diagonal line at a 45 degree angle from corner to corner. Sew 1/4" on both sides of the line. Cut on the line. You will have two half square triangle units. Press each unit open with the seam going in the direction of the darkest fabric.

Cut here

Quarter Square Triangles

Quarter square triangles are made by determining the finished size of the square needed and adding 1-1/4" to that measurement. For example, if you need quarter square triangles that will finish at 3," you must begin with squares that measure 4-1/4."

Place the two squares together with the right sides facing each other and the edges aligned. Draw a line from corner to corner on the wrong side of the lightest fabric and sew 1/4" on each side of the line. Cut on the line, open the square and press the seam allowance to the darkest side of the square. Cut the square on the diagonal again as shown in the illustration below. Open the units and press. Half of the quarter square triangles will be a mirror image of the others.

Cut here
Cut here

If you like, you can make units that have quarter-square triangles on the top portion and a triangle on the bottom or you can make pinwheels by sewing the quarter squares together. The measurements follow the same rules as above.

Flying Geese

One way to make the flying geese units is by determining how large one wants the unit. For example, let's say we want it to measure 3" x 6" as a finished size. We would cut a 7 1/4" square and cut the square from corner to corner twice on the diagonals. This makes the "goose" part of the unit. The next step would be to cut four 3 7/8" squares. Cut the squares on the diagonal once. These triangles make the "sky" part of the unit. Sew two "sky" triangles onto one "goose" triangle to complete the unit.

Of course, there are also other methods. Some people foundation piece and some sew squares to rectangles and then trim to make the unit. There are various rulers on the market that take the math out of the whole process. Rulers that come to mind are Eleanor Burns' Quilt in a Day Flying Geese Ruler™ and No Math Flying Geese Ruler™ by Lazy Girl Designs, etc.

Appliqué

Just as with any other part of the quilt-making process, there are no shortages on methods. There is the needle turn method that involves turning under a small amount of seam allowance as you sew. It is advantageous to use a longer needle made especially for the appliqué process. After knotting your thread, bring the needle up from the back of the fabric to the front. Take very small stitches and push the seam allowance under with the needle as you sew the piece to the background.

Using a buttonhole stitch is also an accepted method of appliqué. To make buttonhole stitches, make a knot in your thread. Working from left to right, bring the needle up from the reverse side of the fabric. Sink the needle in the fabric 1/8" straight up from the position at which you began. Bring the needle out of the fabric 1/8" straight down, looping the thread beneath the needle point. Keep your stitches about 1/8" apart and make them about 1/8" long. The stitches need to be very even in order to look good. Sew around the entire piece using this stitch.

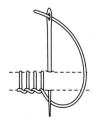

To machine appliqué, cut the pieces using templates and do not add a seam allowance. Satin stitch around the entire piece using thread that matches the fabric. Some people prefer to use a fusible web and press the pieces in place, then stitch around the edge of each fused piece. When doing this, one needs to follow each manufacturer's directions. Another option is to trace all the pattern pieces onto freezer paper. Iron the freezer paper patterns onto the fabric and cut out the pieces. Be sure to add and turn under the seam allowance. After stitching the pieces in

place, cut the fabric from behind the appliqué work. Remove the excess fabric and the freezer paper.

Hints:

When pressing, follow the path of least resistance. The general rule is to press the seams towards the darkest fabric. That doesn't always work. Sometimes one needs to press the seams open to make the block work.

When the pattern calls for a 45 degree triangle to be cut at 3-7/8," that triangle should measure 3-7/8" on the two equal sides.

When there are many pieces with bias edges (such as diamonds), it is best to sew the seams a scant 1/4".

Her granddaughter, Elizabeth Smith of Grandview, Missouri, owns Flower Basket, made by Ollie Elizabeth Marshall of the state of Virginia in the 1930s.

Great Circle pieced by Mary Andrews, Kansas City, Missouri.

GREAT CIRCLE

April 11, 1956
12" finished block

Author's note: I am going to recommend that one use the templates given for this block. There are some odd measurements included because the block has been redrafted to a 12" square.

Fabric needed: background, green, 1 medium print, 1 medium dark print and a dark.

From the background fabric, cut 1 square using template A, one triangle using template D, two triangles using template B and two strips using template C.

From the dark fabric, cut 1 triangle using template D and 2 triangles using template F.

From the green fabric, cut four diamonds using template E.

From the medium print, cut 8 diamonds using template E.

From the medium dark print, cut four diamonds using template E.

Sew a green E diamond to a medium print E diamond.

Step into the museum and view a reproduction of one of the paddle wheels from the Steamboat Arabia. The Arabia was built at the Pringle Boat-Building Company in Brownsville, Pennsylvania, with two paddle wheels, one on each side of the boat. These great circles had covers over them. The boat could carry around 400 tons of cargo when fully loaded but would still only need about 4 1/2 feet of water to float. If you could save up $3, you could claim a spot on the lower deck to sleep. If you were in the money, you could get a cabin for $10 and have all of your meals prepared for you in the dining room.

Press the seams toward the darkest fabric.

Then sew a medium print E diamond to a medium dark print E diamond.

Press the seams towards the darkest fabric.

Sew the two rows together to make a large E diamond. Make four of these large diamonds.

Stitch a background B triangle to the top part of a large E diamond as shown.

Now add another large diamond.

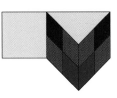

Next add the background A square.

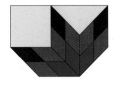

Then add the third large diamond.

Add the remaining B triangle next.

Now sew on the last E diamond.

Add the C strips to the basket as shown.

Press the seams connecting the four diamond units open. You will have less bulk in the seams.

Next sew on the dark D triangle to the base of the basket.

Sew the background D triangle to the basket to complete the block.

Sew the F pieces to the C strips.

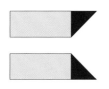

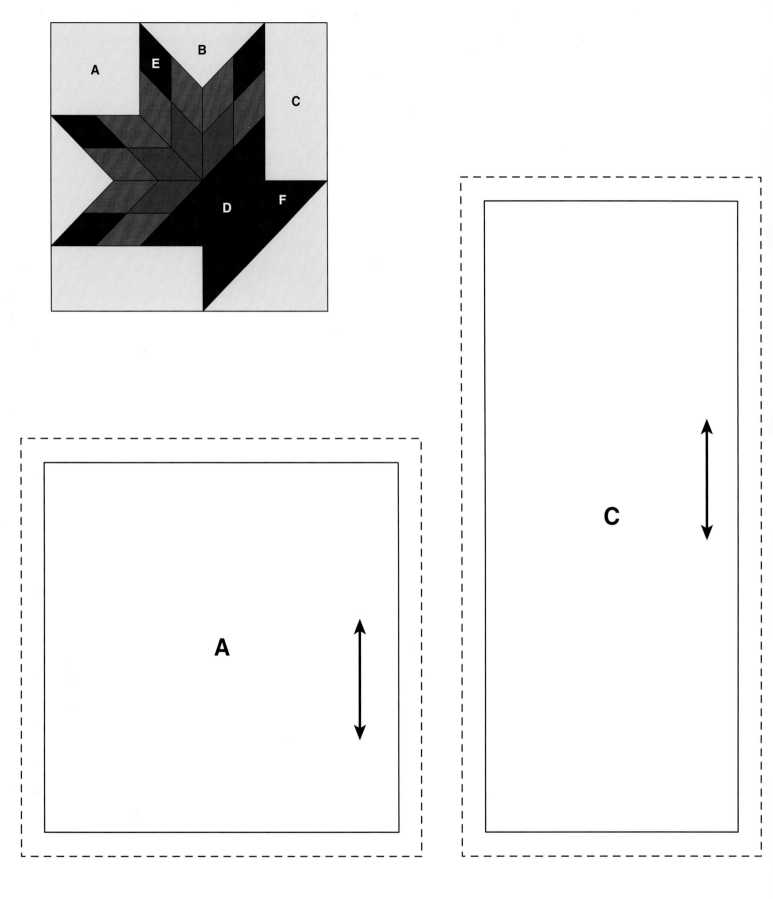

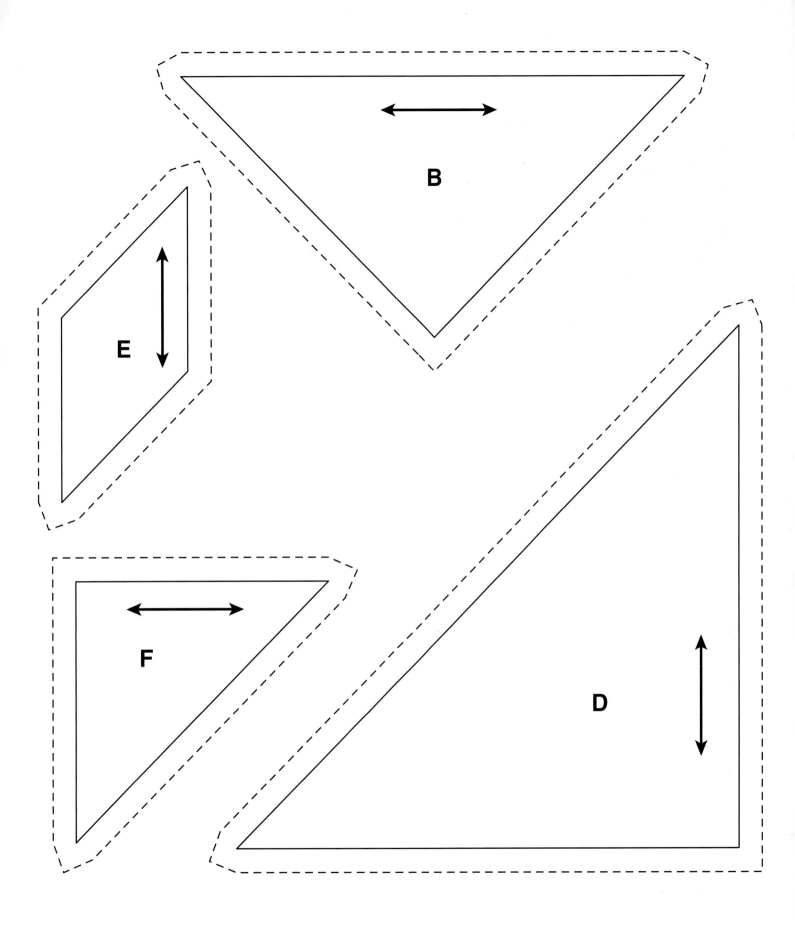

B

E

F

D

Basket of Daisies appliquéd by Margaret Falen, Grain Valley, Missouri.

BASKET OF DAISIES

Original Design by Edie McGinnis
12" finished block

Fabric needed: Background fabric, green, yellow or contrasting color for the flower centers, dark for the basket, green pearl cotton thread, fabric for flower petals.

Use your favorite method of appliqué. If appliquéing by hand, add 1/2" seam allowance.

From the dark fabric, cut one basket and two 1-1/8" x 8" bias strips for the handle.

From the green fabric, cut 11 leaves.

From the yellow or contrasting color, cut four circles for the flower centers.

From the fabric you are using for flower petals, cut 29 large petals and four small petals.

Cut a 13" square of the background fabric. Fold the background fabric in fourths and finger press a crease at each fold line.

Trace the placement diagram onto the background fabric. This is best accomplished by using a light box or by taping the

A basket or jar of wildflowers might have decorated many a pioneer table, adding a bit of beauty to the household. 1856 was a time when chores were difficult. Found in the cargo of the Arabia were 14 cast iron sad irons. This heavy cordless iron was heated on the cook stove or in the fireplace in order to be hot enough to be of any use. Of course, one had to be careful and test the temperature of the iron. You could tell the heat was about right if after licking your finger the saliva would sizzle as you barely touched the iron's surface.

placement diagram to a window. Put the background square over the diagram and trace the pattern using a fine line mechanical pencil. Use the lines you finger pressed in place to center the basket.

Appliqué the basket handle pieces in place beginning with the back portion. Add the bottom of the basket.

Embroider the stems for the leaves using green pearl cotton.

Appliqué the leaves and flower petals in place.

After appliquéing the petals that make up the partially opened bud, add the green sepal. (That is the cup like piece that covers the four petals.)

Add the flower centers to complete the block.

Trim the block to measure 12-1/2."

To create full-size
placement diagram,
tape together diagram
on this page and the
following page.

E

F

D

A

19

20

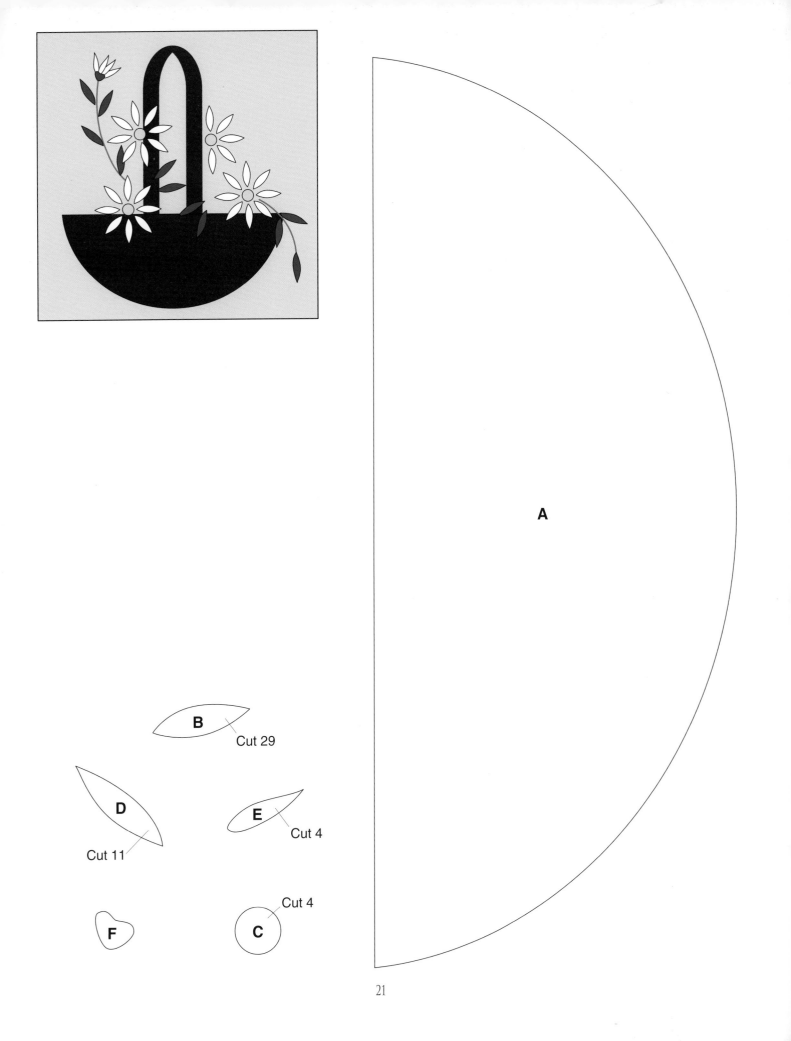

B

Cut 29

D

Cut 11

E

Cut 4

Cut 4

F

C

A

21

May Basket pieced by Jan Keeler, Independence, Missouri.

THE MAY BASKET

July 2, 1941
12" finished block

Fabric needed: background and dark.

From the dark fabric, cut four basket handles using template D, eight 2-7/8" triangles (template C), and four 4-7/8" triangles (template A).

From the background fabric, cut eight 4-7/8" triangles (template A) and eight 2-1/2" squares (template B).

Following the placement diagram, appliqué each basket handle onto a background 4-7/8" triangle (template A).

Sew each background 2-1/2" square (template B) to a dark C triangle.

Children used to make May baskets and hang them from doorknobs to celebrate the beginning of summer. A plethora of doorknobs made of both ceramic and porcelain, keys of every shape and size, locks and door handles, hinges and screws and deadbolts were found in the cargo of the Arabia.

Sew the BC units to a dark A triangle as shown.

Add a background A triangle to the base of the basket.

Now add the A triangle that has the handle appliquéd to complete the unit. You will need to make four of these units.

When the four units are finished, sew them together as shown to complete the block.

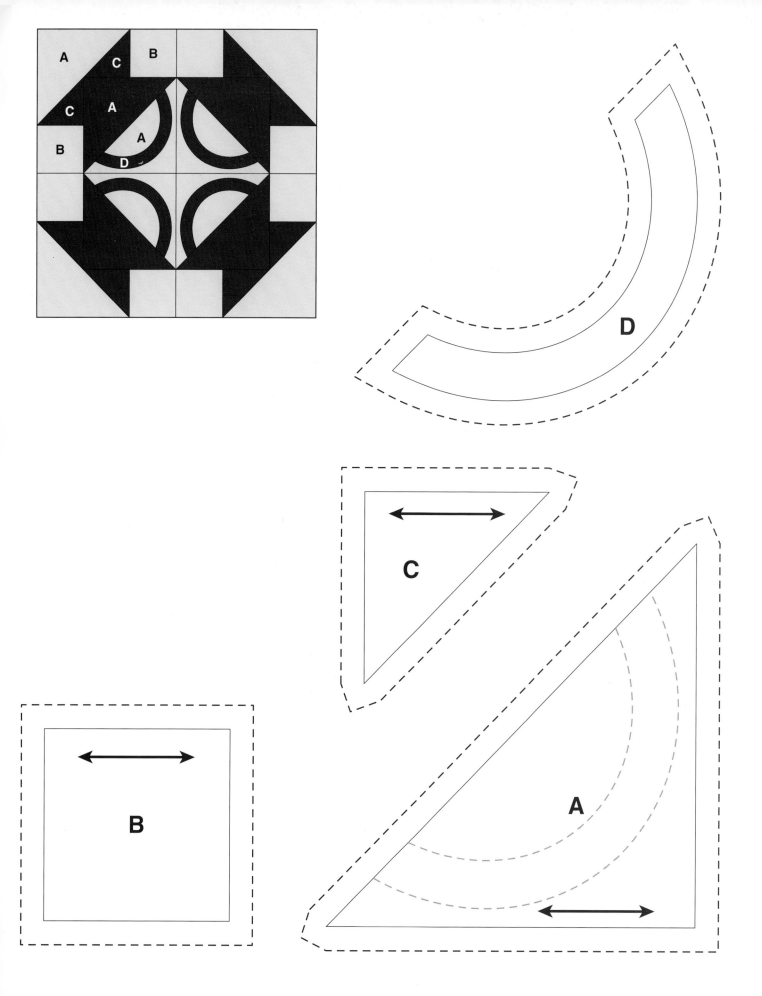

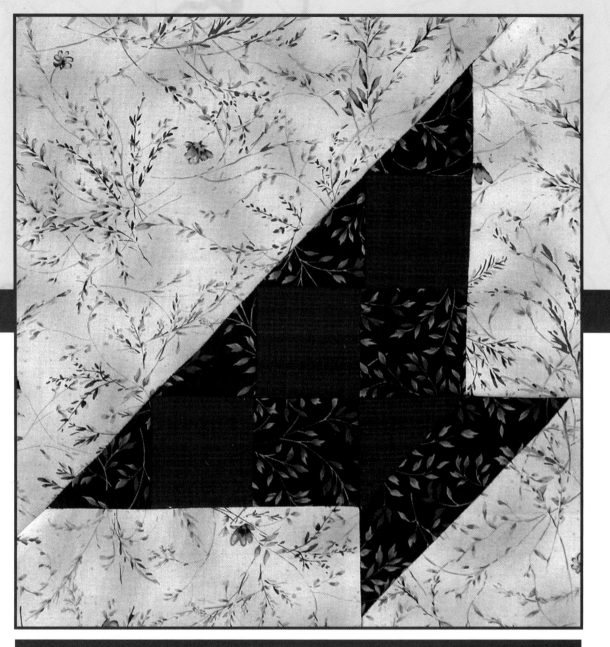

Grandmother's Basket pieced by Rosemary Garten, Independence, Missouri.

GRANDMOTHER'S BASKET

March 2, 1932
12" finished block

Fabric needed: background, medium and dark.

From the background fabric, cut one 12-7/8" triangle (no template is given), one strip using template B, one strip using template Br and one triangle using template C.

From the medium fabric, cut three 2-1/2" squares (template E) and one 2-7/8" triangle (template D).

From the dark fabric, cut two 2-7/8" squares. Cut the squares from corner to corner making four triangles or use template D, two 2-1/2" squares (template E) and one piece using template A.

Sew a dark D triangle to a medium square and add a dark square.

Sew this row to the Br strip.

Remedies for various illnesses were packed along with the other freight. One of my grandmother's favorites was in one of the boxes. Twenty-four bottles of castor oil were found along with "Nerve and Bone Lineament." Many bottles shaped like test tubes containing various unidentified medicines and tins of pills were found. If the illness was very serious, frontiersmen frequently called on the local barber. Tools of his trade, such as lancets for bleeding bad humors from the body, were also on board.

Sew a medium D triangle to the dark A piece. Then add the background C triangle, making a square as shown.

Add the B strip to the side of the unit.

Sew the square to the row with the Br strip you have just made.

Sew the two portions together as shown to complete the lower part of the basket.

Now sew a dark D triangle to a medium E square. Add a dark E square.

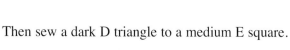

Then sew a dark D triangle to a medium E square.

Finish the block by adding the background 12-7/8" triangle.

Sew these two rows together and add a dark D triangle to the top, as shown.

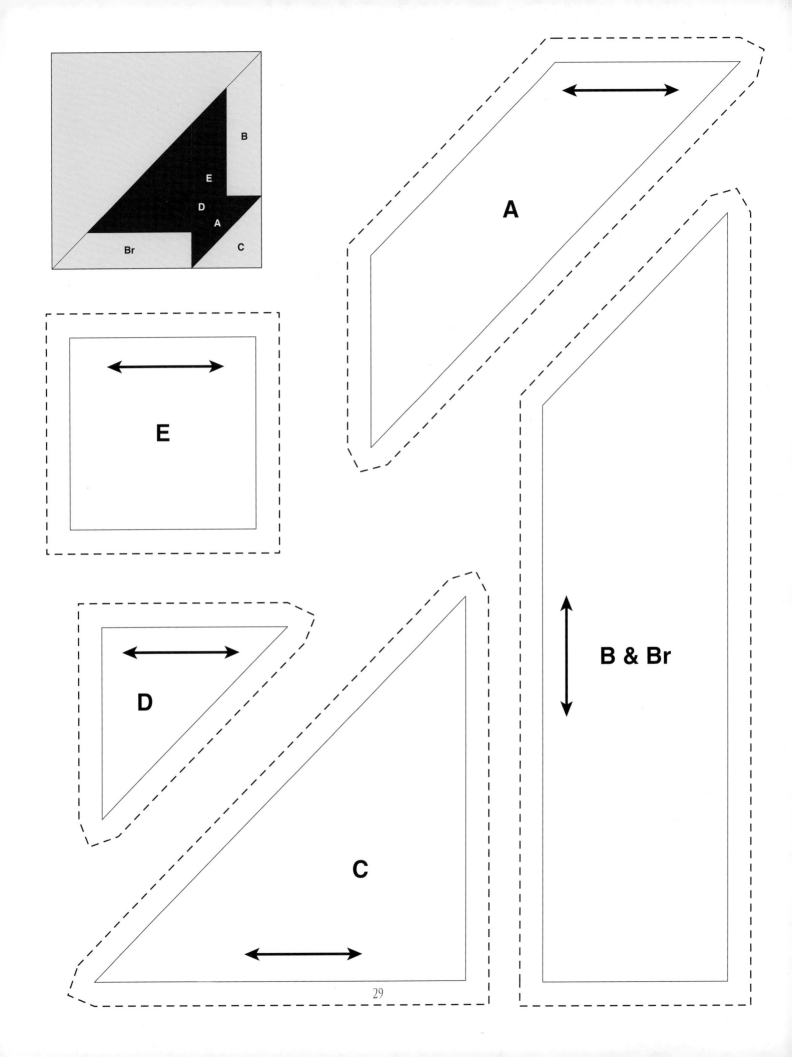

A

E

B & Br

D

C

Br

B

29

Barb's Basket appliquéd by Dee Clevenger, Independence, Missouri.

BARB'S BASKET

Original Design by Edie McGinnis
12" finished block

Fabric needed: background, stripes, green, dark red, print and burgundy.

From the background fabric, cut one 13" square.

Use your favorite method of appliqué when making this block and remember to add 1/4" seam allowance if appliquéing by hand.

From the striped fabric, cut one basket base using template A, two 1-1/4" x 8" bias strips for the handle and one 1" x 12" bias strip for the trim on the basket.

From the print fabric, cut four flowers. You will need to cut two small flowers using template F-2 and two large flowers using template F-1.

From the burgundy fabric, cut four flower centers, two using template D and two using template E.

Cut 15 berries using template B from the dark red fabric.

As the Hawleys unpacked boxes filled with fragile glassware, they sometimes found the packing material as interesting as the contents of the boxes. Many items were packed in nutmeg, almonds or pumpkin seeds. This served a dual purpose. Not only were the items kept from breaking but valuable nuts and spices were added to the cargo without taking up more space.

Using templates L1 through L4, cut the leaves from the green fabric. You will also need to cut a 3/8" x 26" bias strip from the green for the flower and berry stems.

Trace the placement diagram onto the background fabric. This is best accomplished by placing a copy of the diagram on a light box and taping the background fabric down while you are tracing.

Pin the basket base in place and sew the two sides and the bottom in place. Leave the top of the basket open for the moment.

Tuck the leaf and berry stems in place. Fold the fabric for the stems in half, stitch in place by sewing on the top then flipping the fold over the seam and sewing down the remaining loose side.

Sew leaf L1 in place. Pin and stitch the basket handle pieces in place next. Stitch the piece that appears to be the far side of the handle in place first. Then add the trim to the basket. Close the top of the basket as you stitch the trim in place. Now appliqué the last part of the basket handle in place.

Pin the remaining pieces in place and appliqué.

Trim the square to 12-1/2" to complete the block.

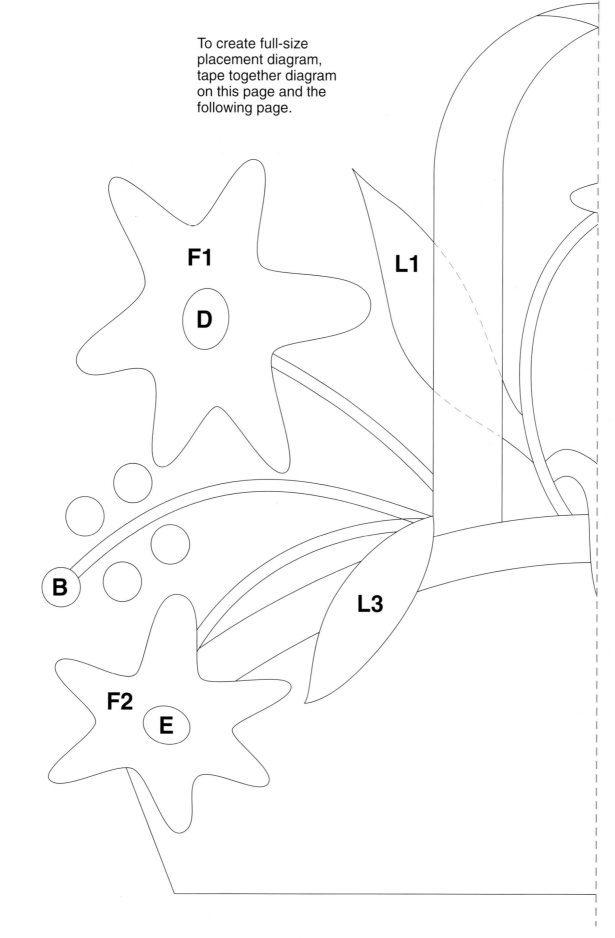

To create full-size
placement diagram,
tape together diagram
on this page and the
following page.

F1

D

L1

B

L3

F2

E

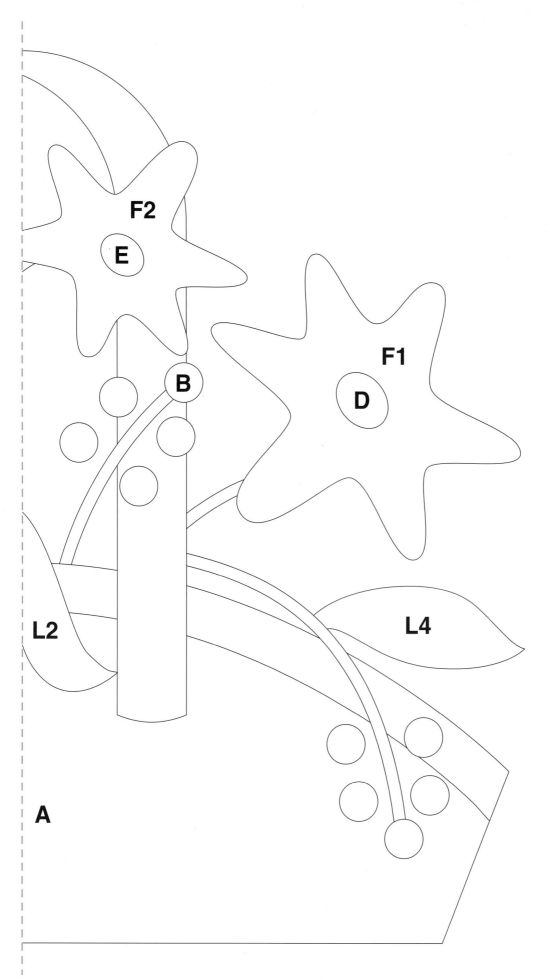

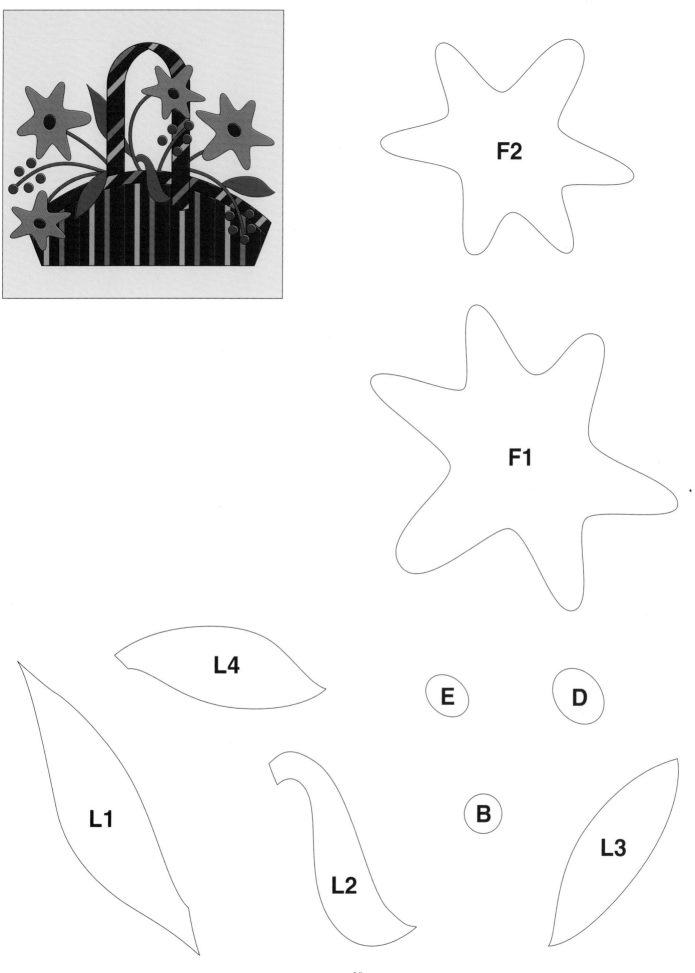

F2

F1

L4

E

D

L1

B

L2

L3

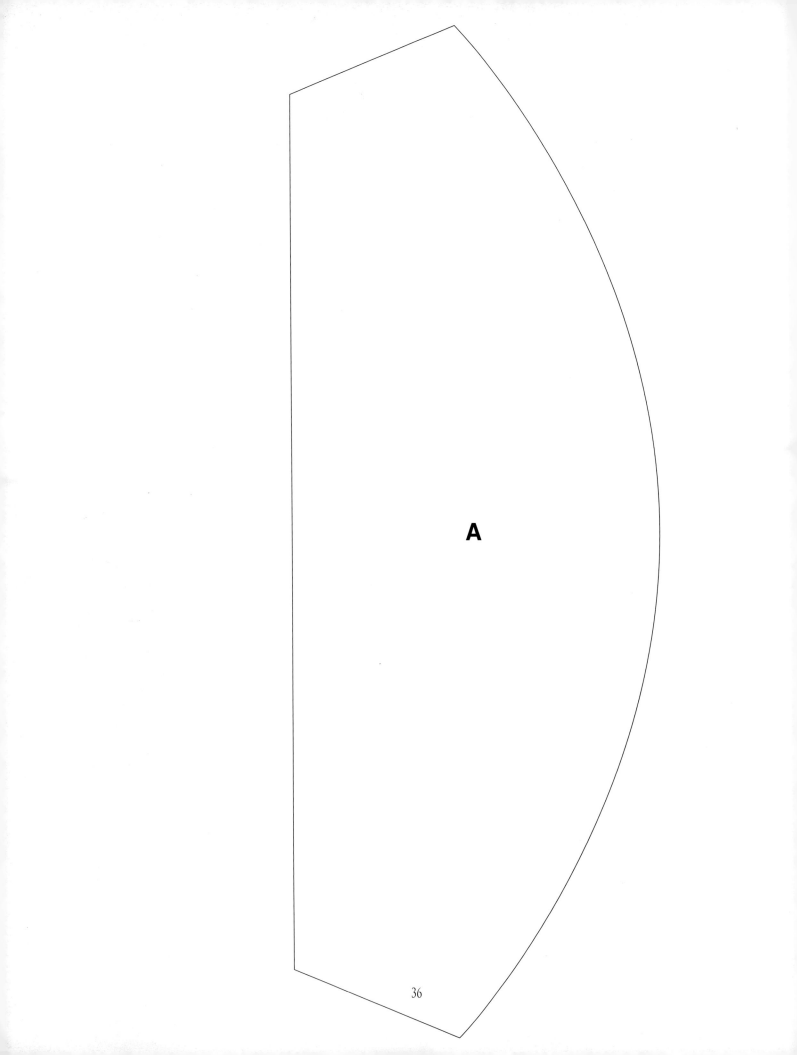

A

36

Owned by the author, Edie McGinnis, Kansas City, Missouri, this Cherry Basket
quilt was made of pink solid and print 1930s fabric and was quilted by hand.
The maker and quilter are unknown.

Cherry Basket pieced by Jan Keeler, Independence, Missouri.

CHERRY BASKET

October 24, 1928
12" finished block

Fabric needed: background, light and dark.

From the background fabric, cut one 10-7/8" triangle, two 2-1/2" x 8-1/2" strips (template B) and one 4-7/8" triangle.

From the light fabric, cut five 2-7/8" squares or ten triangles using template D.

From the dark fabric, cut nine 2-7/8" squares, subcut four of the squares into 8 triangles by cutting from corner to corner on the diagonal (you will have one triangle left over) OR cut 17 triangles using template D and one bias strip 1 1/4" x 18".

For this block, one needs to make ten half-square triangle units. You may cut out and sew the individual triangles together to make the half-square triangle units or you may use the squares and draw a line from corner to corner on the reverse side of the five medium squares. Place a light square atop a dark square and sew 1/4" on each side of the line. Cut along the line, open the pieces and press toward the darker fabric. You should have ten half-square triangle units.

Thirty-six glass jars of cherries, light and dark, were found preserved in brandy. The cherries had been shipped from France so the ladies on the frontier could offer up a lovely cherry pie for special occasions. If one didn't care for cherries, one could also choose from apples, blackberries, currants, gooseberries or rhubarb. Each type of fruit was packed in a glass bottle, then sealed with a cork.

To make the basket, sew one dark D triangle to the lightest side of a half-square triangle unit as shown.

Add three more half-square triangle units to make the bottom row of the basket.

Row two is made up of one dark D triangle and three half-square triangle units.

Row three is made of one dark D triangle and two half-square triangle units.

Row four uses one dark D triangle and one half-square triangle unit.

Sew the rows together as shown and add a dark D triangle to the top to finish this part of the basket.

Now sew a dark D triangle onto the end of each B strip.

Sew each B strip to the basket as shown.

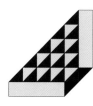

Add the C triangle to complete this part of the block,

Using the placement diagram, trace the basket handle position onto the background 10 7/8" triangle.

Press a 1/4" seam allowance under on both sides of the bias strip.

Appliqué the strip in place by following the pencil line you marked on the triangle.

Sew the two halves together to complete the block.

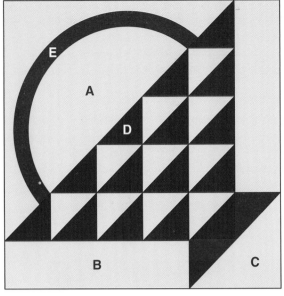

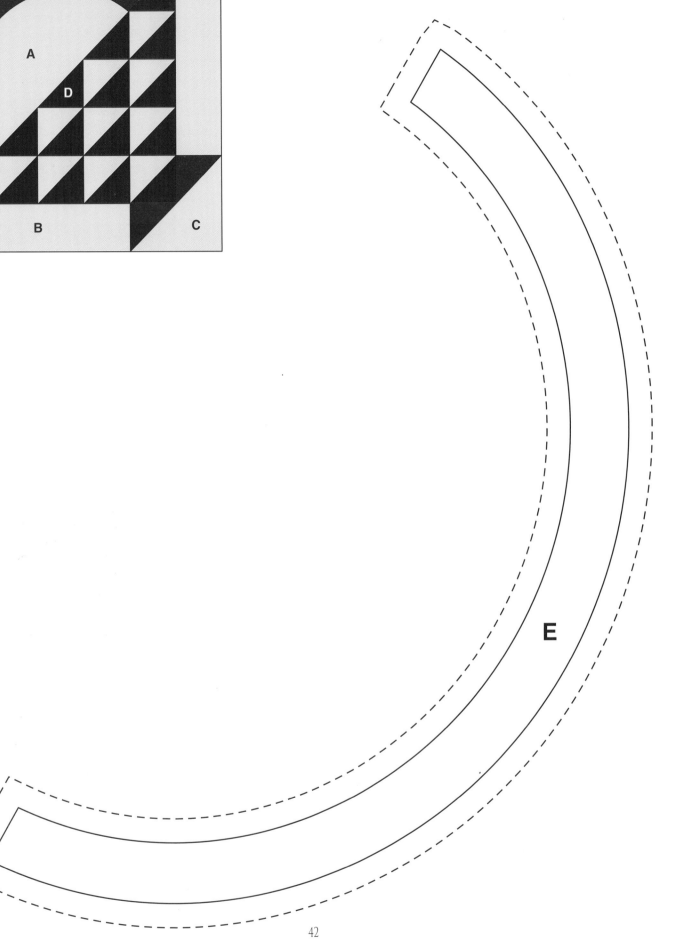

E

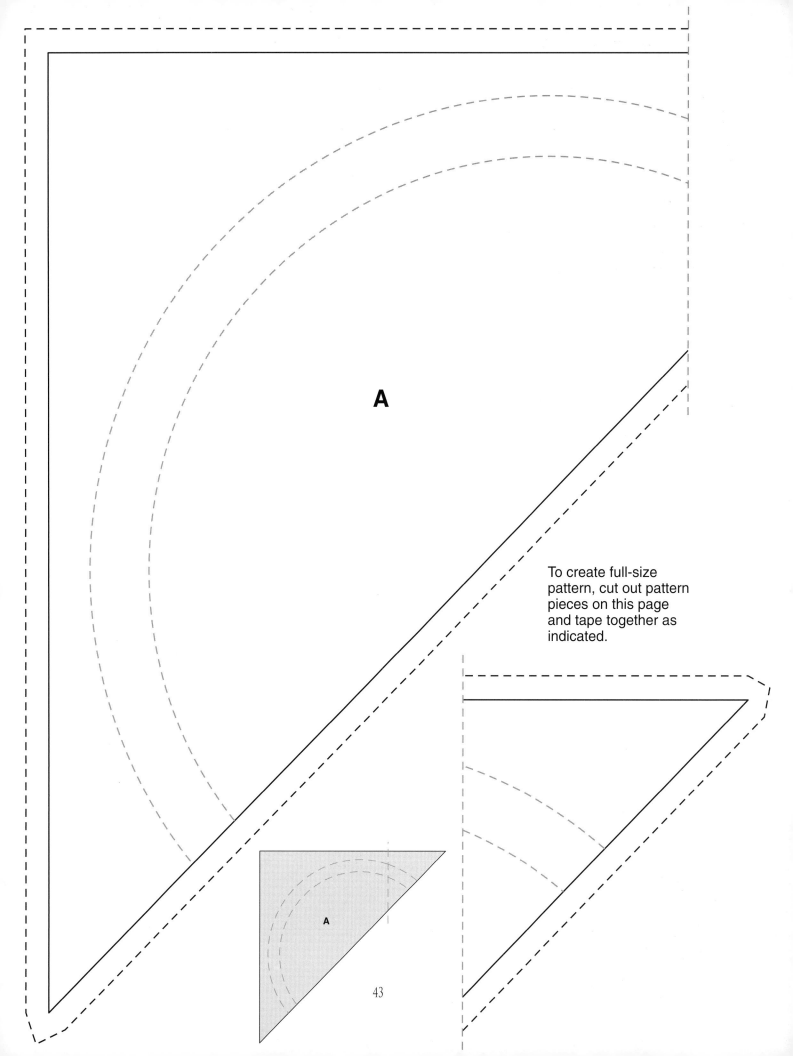

A

To create full-size pattern, cut out pattern pieces on this page and tape together as indicated.

A

43

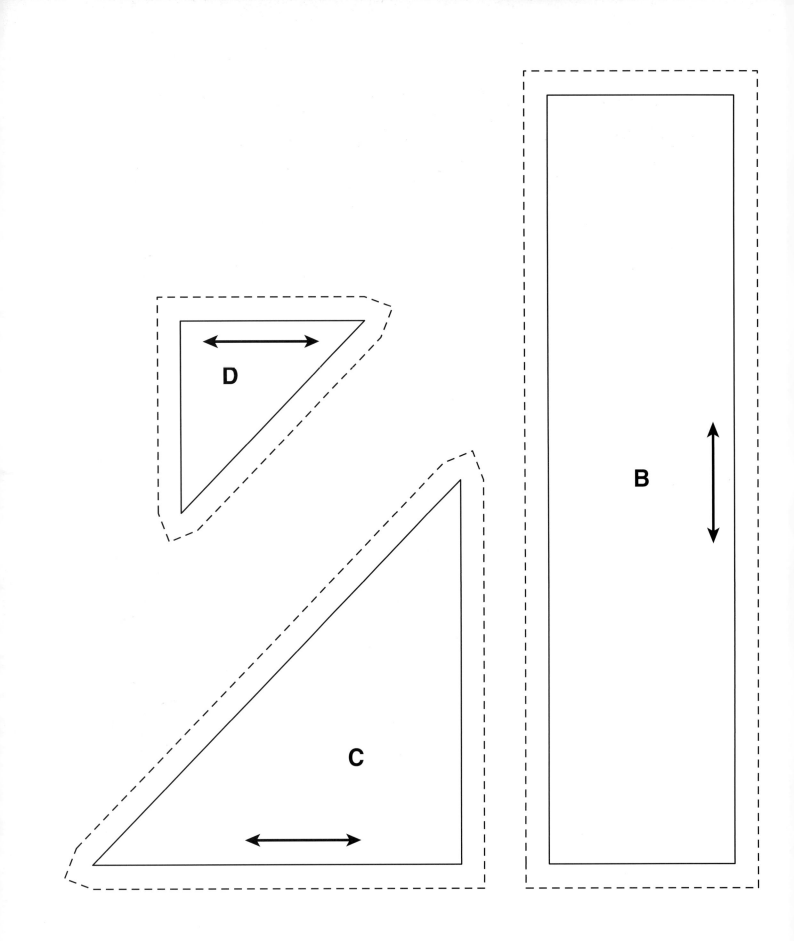

Janette Luehring of Prairie Village, Kansas, owns this Flower Basket quilt.
The quilt was purchased from an antique shop in Atchison, Kansas, in October of 2001.
The maker and quilter are unknown.

Flower Basket pieced by Bami Drinkwater, Independence, Missouri.

F L O W E R B A S K E T

July 31, 1935
12" finished block

Fabric needed: background, four prints and a dark.

Author's Note: I suggest you use templates because the pieces may be of an odd size because the pattern has been redrafted to a 12" finished size block.

From the background fabric, cut two rectangles using template C, one triangle using template D, two triangles using template B and one square using template A.

From the four prints, cut 4 diamonds using template F.

From the dark fabric, cut one triangle using template D and two triangles using template E.

Sew a background B triangle to a print F diamond.

It is very important to pin when piecing quilts. The women who were quilting or making garments on the frontier would have sorely missed the pins found aboard the sunken Arabia. The salvagers found 10,000 brass straight pins and 5,000 steel needles. Both seemed to be very large in comparison to the fine betweens and the ballpoint pins the quilter has in her sewing basket today.

Basket of Oranges pieced and appliquéd by Alta Short, Independence, Missouri.

BASKET OF ORANGES

July 16, 1930
12" finished block

Fabric needed: background, light, dark, orange and green.

From the background fabric, cut two 2-1/2" x 10-1/2" strips (template B), one 4-7/8" triangle (template C) and one piece using template A.

From the light fabric, cut one 2-1/2" square (template E) and five 2-7/8" triangles (template D).

From the dark fabric, cut eleven 2-7/8" triangles, (template D) and one basket handle using template H or a bias strip 1-1/4" x 18".

From the green fabric, cut nine leaves using template I.

From the orange fabric, cut one large orange using template G and four smaller oranges using template F.

To make the basket, sew the five light D triangles to five dark D triangles to make five half-square triangle units.

Oranges were rare on the frontier and continued to be difficult to obtain until refrigerated trucks and freight cars came on the scene to transport the fruit in a timely manner. One of the fruits easily transported aboard a steamship was tinned peaches. An open tin was found in the dining area of the Arabia. There was no beautiful label but the can had been opened and the peaches had been served to the passengers.

Sew a dark D triangle to a half-square triangle unit then add another half-square triangle unit. End the row with the 2-1/2" square.

The next row is made of one dark triangle sewn to a half-square triangle. Add another half-square triangle.

The third row is a dark triangle sewn to one half-square triangle unit.

Sew the rows together and add a dark D triangle to the top.

Use the placement diagram to mark the position of the handle, the oranges and the leaves on the background A piece. This is easily accomplished by making a copy of the diagram on a copy machine, taping it to a light box, placing your fabric on top and tracing the positions lightly onto the fabric. Appliqué the handle in place.

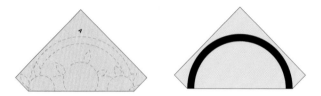

Position and pin the oranges and leaves onto the block and appliqué all but two of the leaves in place.

Sew the two halves of the basket together.

Stitch on the background C triangle.

Now sew a dark triangle onto each of the B strips. Sew each of the B strips onto the basket as shown.

Appliqué the last two leaves in place to complete the block.

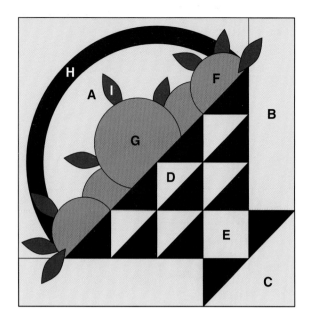

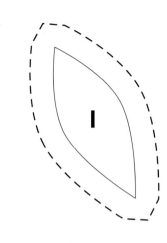

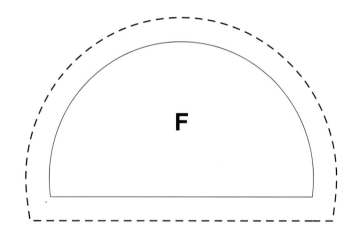

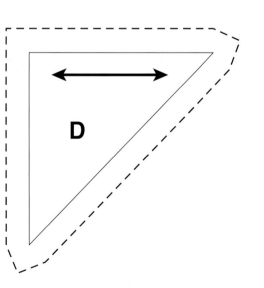

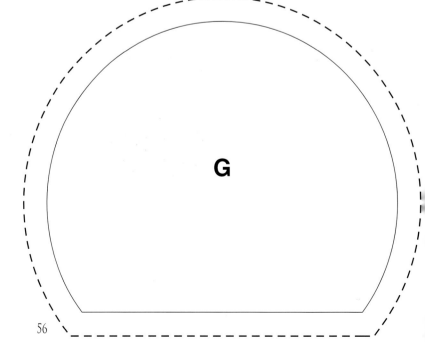

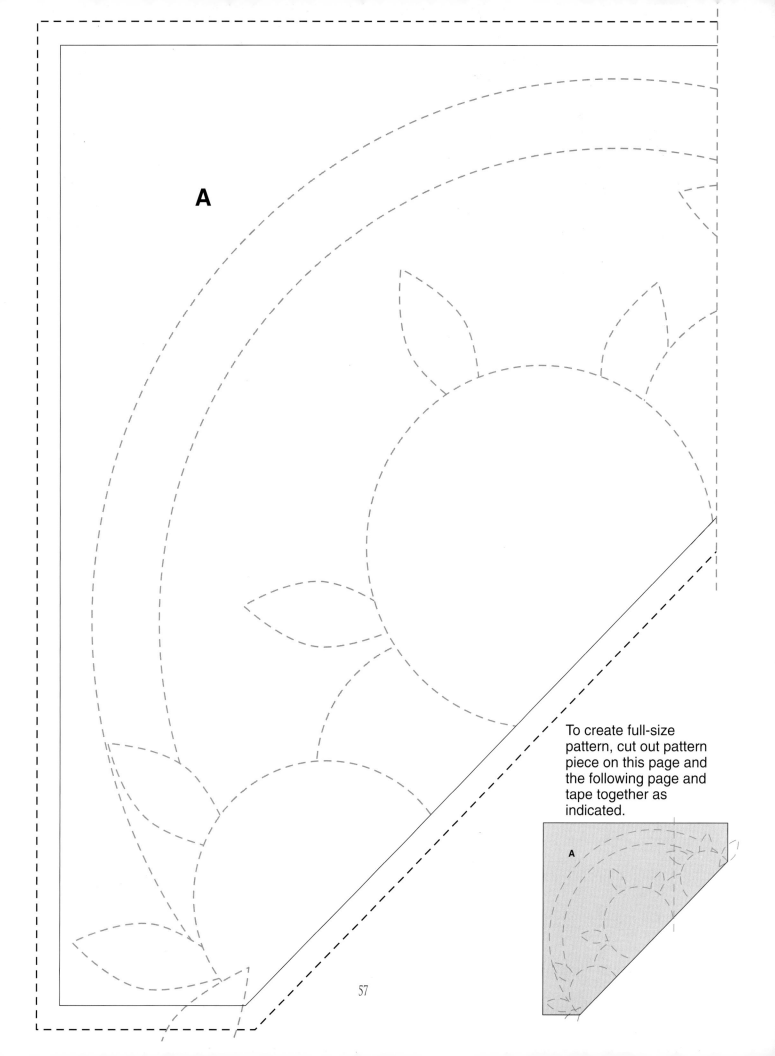

A

To create full-size pattern, cut out pattern piece on this page and the following page and tape together as indicated.

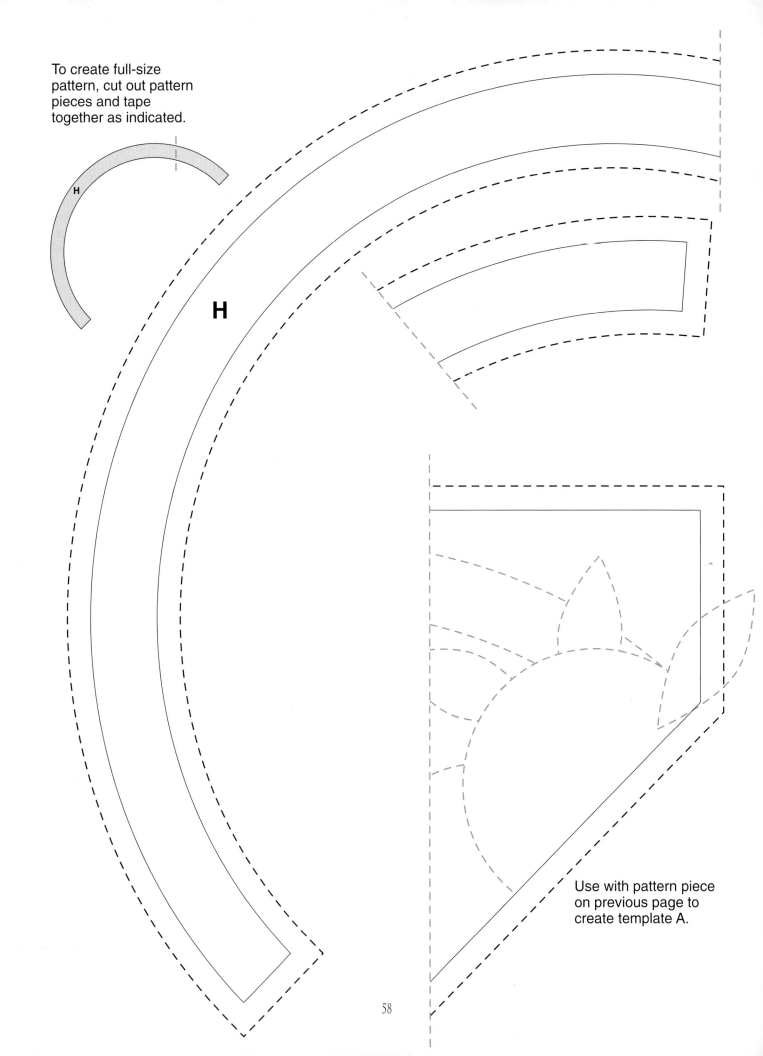

To create full-size pattern, cut out pattern pieces and tape together as indicated.

H

H

Use with pattern piece on previous page to create template A.

58

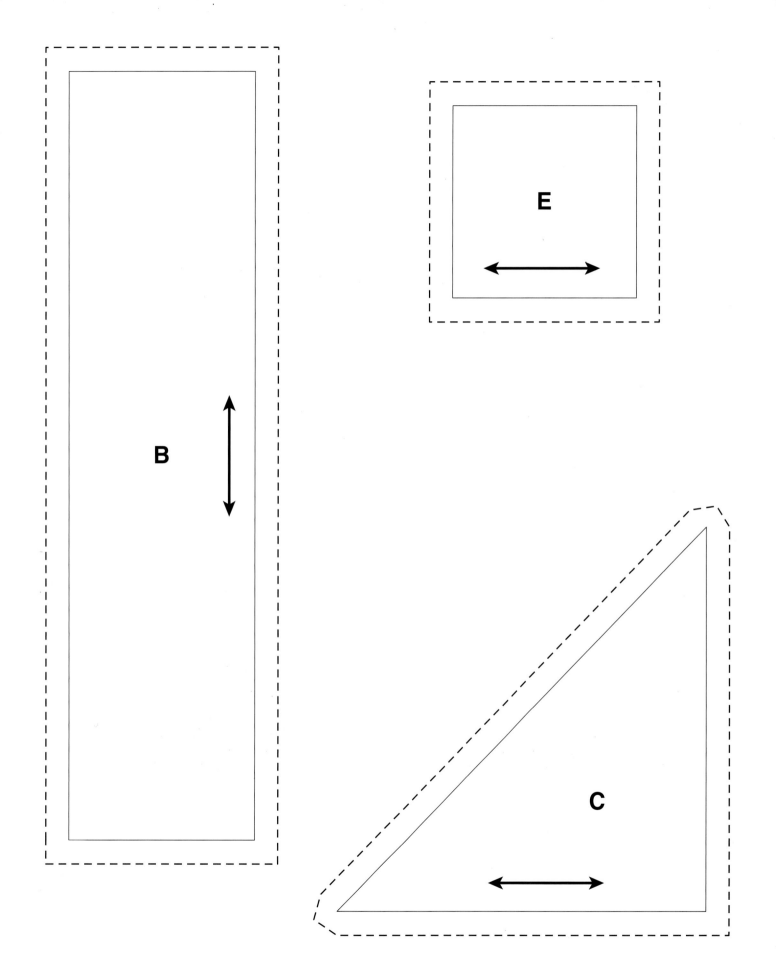

59

Hanging Basket pieced by Clara Diaz, Independence, Missouri.

H A N G I N G   B A S K E T

August 11, 1937
12" finished block

Fabric needed: background and dark.

From the background fabric, cut two 1-1/2" squares (template A), two 2-1/2" x 10-1/2" strips (template B), two 2-1/2" x 6-1/2" strips (template C), one 4-7/8" triangle (template D), one 6-7/8" triangle (template G), seven 1-7/8" squares or 14 triangles using template E.

From the dark fabric, cut three 1-1/2" squares (template A), six 1-7/8" squares or 12 triangles using template E, one 8-7/8" square cut from corner to corner (template H) and one 2-7/8" square cut on the diagonal or cut two triangles using template F.

For the handle of the basket, you will need to make 12 half-square triangle units. If you cut out the triangles using the templates, sew them together to make the half-square triangle units. If you cut out squares, mark a line on the wrong side of the background fabric from corner to corner and place each light square atop a dark square. Sew 1/4" on each side of the marked line. Cut along the line, open the unit and press each open toward the dark fabric. You should have one background square remaining which needs to be cut from corner to corner on the diagonal.

My grandma and my mom used to have a basket for clothespins that hung from a hook. They would slide the hook along the clothesline and push the basket of pins along so they were always handy. My grandma favored the peg type of clothespins but my mom liked the ones with the spring in them. I was surprised to find that both types of pins were found on the Arabia. Both styles were much larger than the ones that can be found today. I'm sure that had a great deal to do with the size of rope used for clotheslines back in 1856.

Stitch one half-square triangle unit to a dark 1-1/2" square, then add five more half-square triangle units. End the row with a background triangle.

Sew the remaining half-square triangle units together beginning with the one remaining background triangle as shown.

Sew this strip to the 6-7/8" (G) triangle.

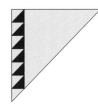

Add the strip that begins with the dark square.

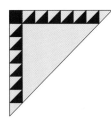

Next sew on the dark 8-7/8" (H) triangle. At this point your block should look like this.

Now sew a dark (F) triangle to the two background 2-1/2" x 6-1/2" (C) strips.

Stitch these to two sides of the bottom of the basket as shown. Add the 4-7/8" (D) triangle to finish the side of the block.

For the upper left hand corner of the block, make a four-patch unit by sewing a dark 1-1/2" square to a background 1-1/2" square. Make two of these and sew them together as shown.

Sew the four-patch unit to one end of one of the 2-1/2" x 10-1/2" (B) strips.

Sew the remaining (B) strip to the top of the block.

Sew the strip containing the four-patch onto the block. Your block should look like this.

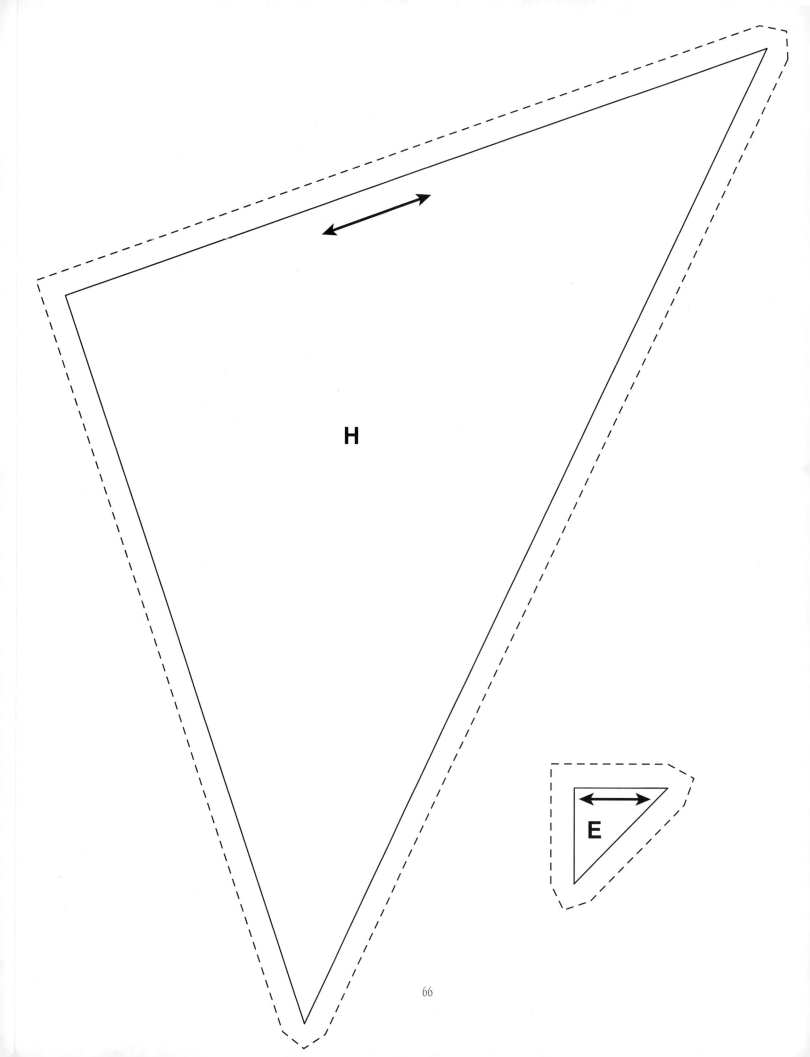

H

E

66

Judy Streu, Liberty, Missouri, owns this orange and white basket quilt. It might be an example of a quilt maker who enjoyed piecing but not appliquéing since the basket is an exact reproduction of the orange basket without the oranges.

The Basket pieced by Karlene Cooper, Kansas City, Missouri.

THE BASKET

April 16, 1938
12" finished block

Fabric needed: background and dark.

From the background fabric, cut 1 triangle using template A, two strips using template B, one triangle using template C, one triangle using template G and 3 triangles using template E.

From the dark fabric, cut two strips using template D, two triangles using template G, one strip using template F and 5 triangles using template E.

To make the bottom row of the basket, sew a background triangle to a dark triangle and add another dark triangle as shown.

Sew the dark F strip to the small background triangle. Add a background G triangle.

Perhaps a basket like this could have been used to hold what few toys pioneer children owned. Although there were 80 wooden doll legs and arms found in the cargo area of the boat, very few toys were found among the passengers' belongings. There were 7 marbles, a tin toy rickshaw, 1 doll shoe and one frozen Charlotte doll made of porcelain. The frozen Charlotte doll holds her arms out from the elbows. Legend has it that Charlotte and her beau, Charley, went to a New Years ball 15 miles from her home. They took the sleigh on this cold, bitter night. Charlotte refused to wrap up in a coat or blanket because she didn't want to wrinkle her lovely dress. As she got colder and complained, Charley offered her his coat, but she refused. By the time they got to the dance, poor, vain Charlotte had frozen to death. It's said Charley died of a broken heart, and both were buried together.

Hicks Basket pieced by Ruby Downing, Oak Grove, Missouri.

HICKS BASKET

March 13, 1940
12" finished block

Fabric needed: background, medium light, medium and dark.

Author's Note: I am going to recommend that one use the templates given for this block. There are some odd measurements included because the block has been redrafted to a 12" square.

From the background fabric, cut one square using template A, two rectangles using template C and one triangle using template D.

From the medium light fabric, cut 8 diamonds using template E.

From the medium fabric, cut 8 diamonds using template E. From the dark fabric, cut two pieces using template F.

Sew a medium light E diamond to a medium E diamond.

Then sew a medium E diamond to a medium light E diamond.

This quilt pattern is credited to a Mr. A.M. Hicks of Isabella, Missouri. He based the pattern on a section of parquet flooring. He must have been quite a mathematician and had an artistic eye as well. Without the aid of a computer, he determined how to make each diamond in the design equal. Had Mr. Hicks lived in 1856, he could have used the drawing implements found on the Arabia. There were dividers, traveling inkwells, slates, slate pencils, around 2,000 nibs for pens and over 500 pencils.

Sew the two rows together to make a large E diamond. Make four of these large E diamonds.

Stitch a background B triangle to the top part of a large E diamond as shown.

Now add another large diamond.

Next add the background A square.

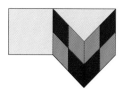

Then add the third large diamond.

Add the remaining B triangle next.

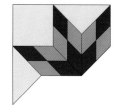

Sew on the last large diamond.

Next sew on one of the dark F pieces to the base of the basket.

Sew the remaining F piece to the background D triangle.

Add the background C strips to the basket as shown.

Sew the FD unit in place to complete the block.

Edie's Basket pieced by Bami Drinkwater, Independence, Missouri.

EDIE'S BASKET

Original Design by Edie McGinnis
12" finished block

Fabric needed: background and dark.

From the background fabric, cut two triangles using template A, one square using template G, one triangle using template D, one piece using template B and one piece using template Br and six triangles using template E.

From the dark fabric, cut six triangles using template E, eight triangles using template C, one triangle using template D, one piece using template F and one piece using template Fr.

To make the basket handle, sew a background E triangle to a dark E triangle as shown. Make three of these units. Make three more units reversing the position of the background fabric as shown.

Sew a C triangle to each of the units. Then sew two sets of three units together.

Of all the artifacts aboard the Arabia, the ones I most covet are the thimbles. There are two basic styles: one has a dimpled top, the other is an open-topped quilting thimble. Most are made of brass, but there were also some silver thimbles among the 469 found. As I read about the thimbles, I discovered they were also used as trade goods with the Native Americans. Sometimes a smaller thimble would be placed inside a larger one, forming a bell. The thimbles were called "tinklers" and used as ornaments on clothing.

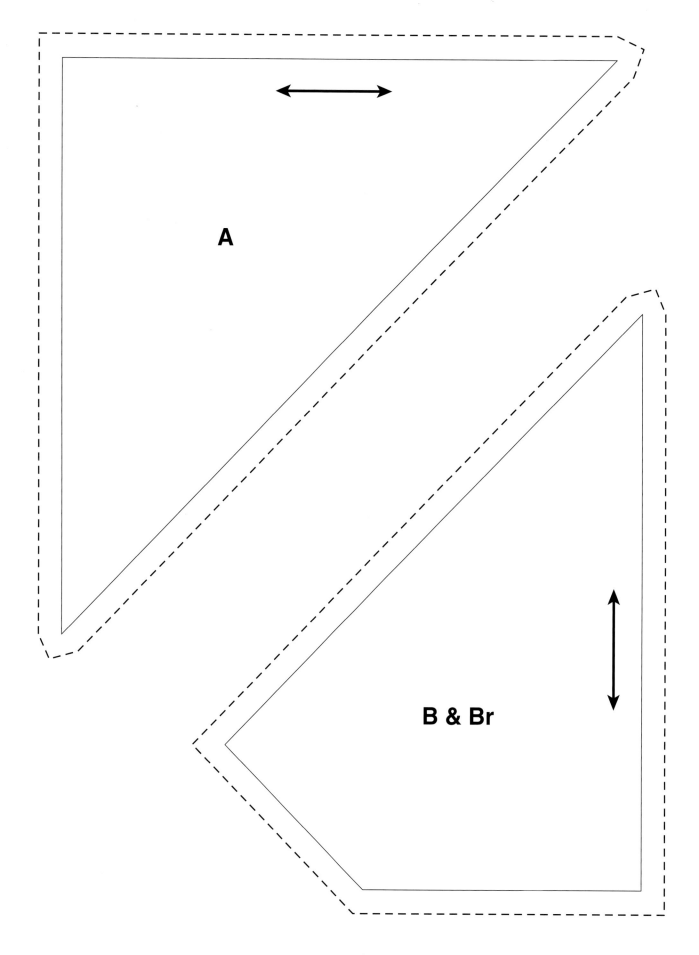

A

B & Br

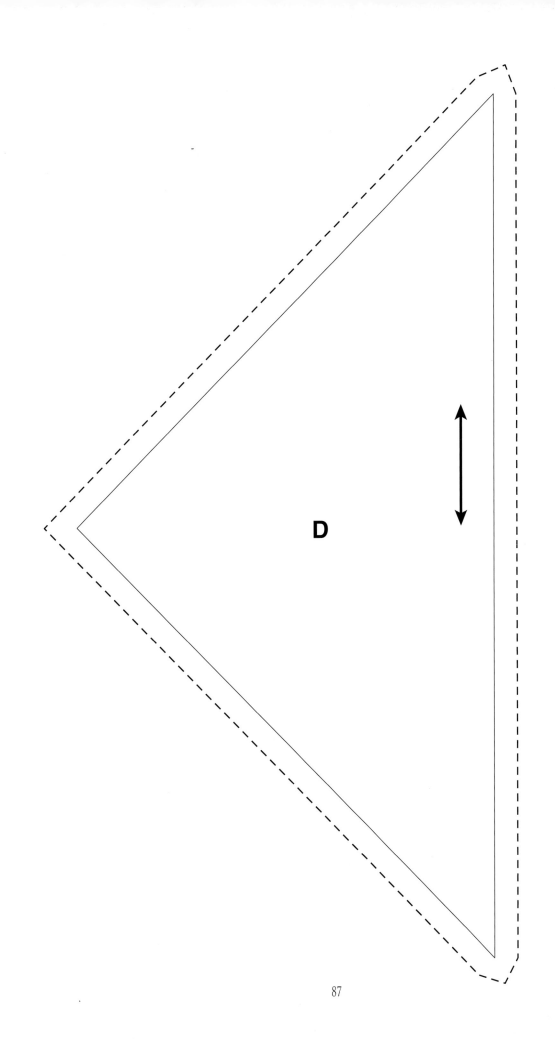

D

The Hicks Flower Basket pieced by Peggy Hutinett, Raytown, Missouri.

THE HICKS FLOWER BASKET

May 14, 1958
12" finished block

Author's note: I am going to recommend that one use the templates given for this block. There are some odd measurements included because the block has been redrafted to a 12" square.

Fabric needed: background, medium light, medium and dark.

From the background fabric, cut 1 square using template A and two triangles using template B

From the dark fabric, cut 1 triangle using template D and 4 diamonds using template C.

From the medium light fabric, cut four diamonds using template C.

From the medium print, cut 8 diamonds using template C.

Sew a medium light C diamond to a medium print C diamond.

Like a bright basket of flowers, thousands upon thousands of buttons shine in the museum. There are plenty of plain white and black ones but also the prettiest plaid and calico buttons you have ever seen. The buttons were made from all types of material: glass, rubber, horn, china, brass and steel.

Sew a medium print C diamond to a dark C diamond.

Sew the two rows together to make a large diamond. Make four of these large diamonds.

Stitch a background B triangle to the top part of a large diamond as shown.

Now add another large diamond.

Next add the background A square.

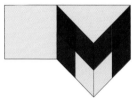

Then add the third large diamond.

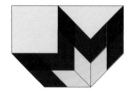

Add the remaining B triangle next.

Now sew on the last large diamond.

Sew on the dark D triangle to the base of the basket to complete the block.

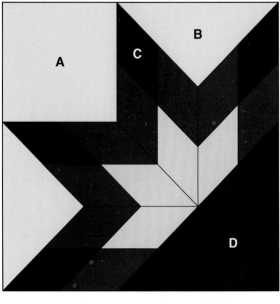

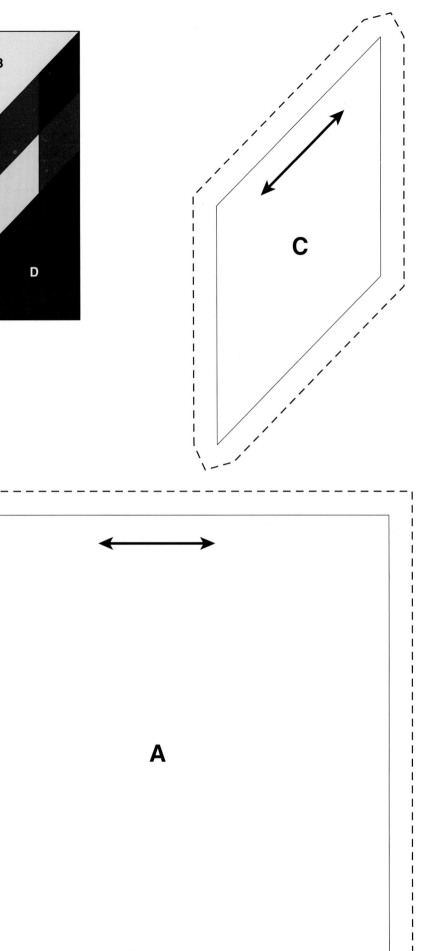

C

A

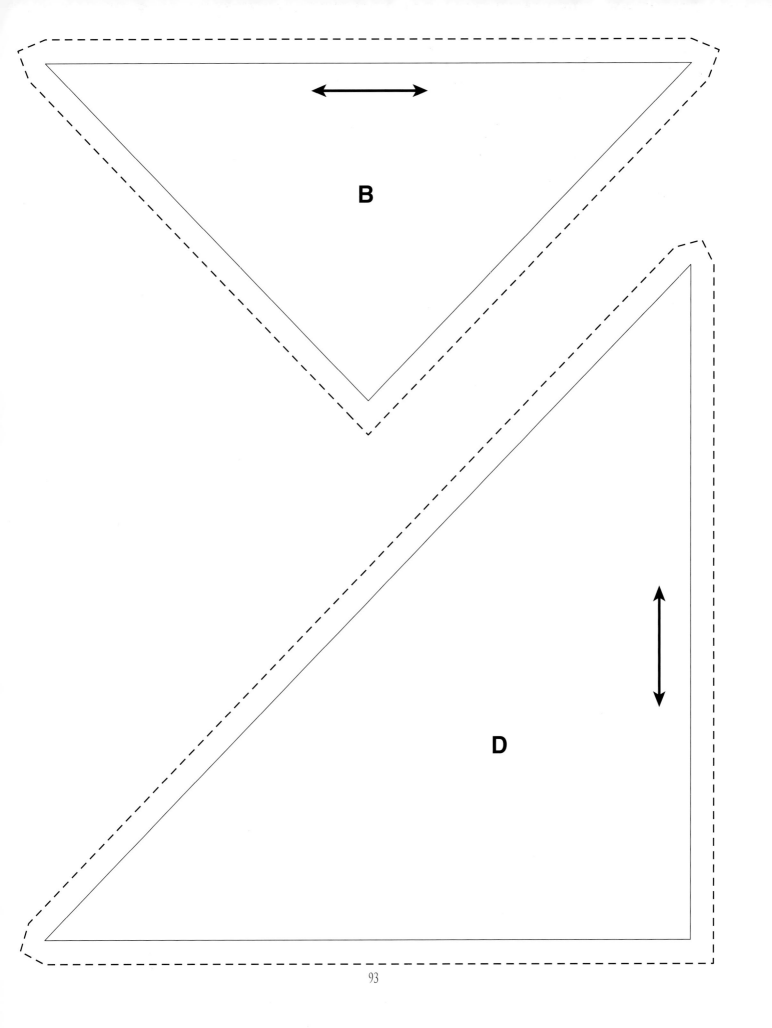

B

D

93

A Basket Quilt in Triangles pieced by Alta Short, Independence, Missouri.

A BASKET QUILT IN TRIANGLES

December 16, 1942
12" finished block

Fabric needed: background and dark.

From the background fabric, cut two 2-1/2" x 8-1/2" strips (template C), one 2-1/2" square (template A), one 4-1/2" triangle (template D), one 8-7/8" triangle (template E) and seven 2-7/8" squares or 14 triangles using template B.

From the dark fabric, cut ten 2-7/8" squares or 20 triangles using template B.

On the seven background squares, mark a line from corner to corner.

Place each background square atop a dark square and sew 1/4" on each side of the marked line. Cut on the line, open each unit and press towards the dark fabric.

The salvaging team found 19 iron bed keys. When I toured the museum, Bob Hawley came in to speak to the group I was with and talked of the bed keys. He asked one little boy what his parents said to him when they tucked him in at night. "Night, night, sleep tight, don't let the bedbugs bite," was the answer. Bob smiled and asked the young man if he knew what that meant. After the child shook his head no, Mr. Hawley explained, "Many beds in 1856 used ropes rather than bedsprings. The bed keys were used to tighten the ropes since they would gradually stretch after use." Mr. Hawley also said there was a bit more to that poem than we ordinarily heard. He said it continued on with, "But if they do, take your shoe and break their little heads in two."

Cut the three remaining dark squares from corner to corner making six triangles.

To construct the handle portion of the block, sew four half-square triangle units together.

Sew the strip to the 8-1/2" triangle (template E).

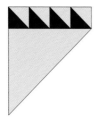

Sew another strip of four half-square triangle units together. Add the background 2-1/2" square to the strip.

Add this strip to the left side of the E triangle.

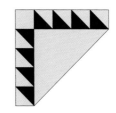

Set this portion of the block aside.

To one dark triangle, sew three half-square triangle units.

Begin the next row with a dark triangle and add two half-square triangle units.

The third row is made by sewing a dark triangle to one half-square triangle unit.

Sew the rows together and add one dark triangle as shown.

Sew this to the unit you set aside earlier. Your block should now look like this.

Sew a dark triangle to each of the two background 8 1/2" strips as shown.

Sew the two strips to the block.

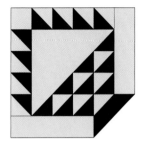

Add the remaining background triangle as shown to complete the block.

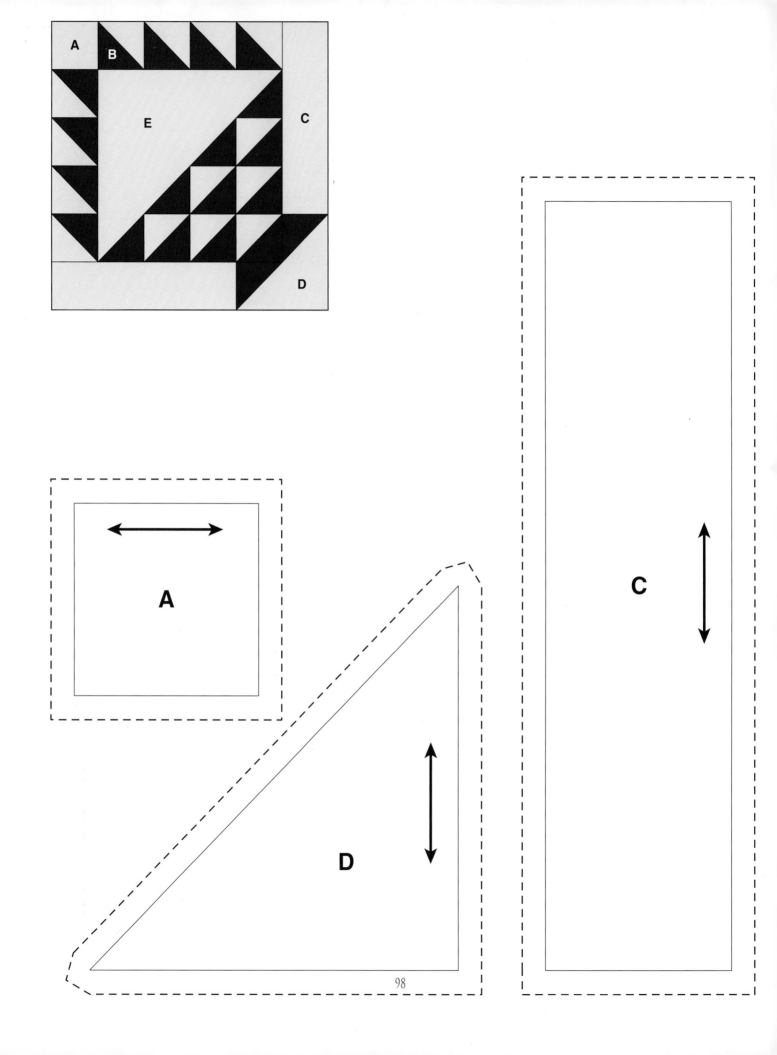

A

C

D

98

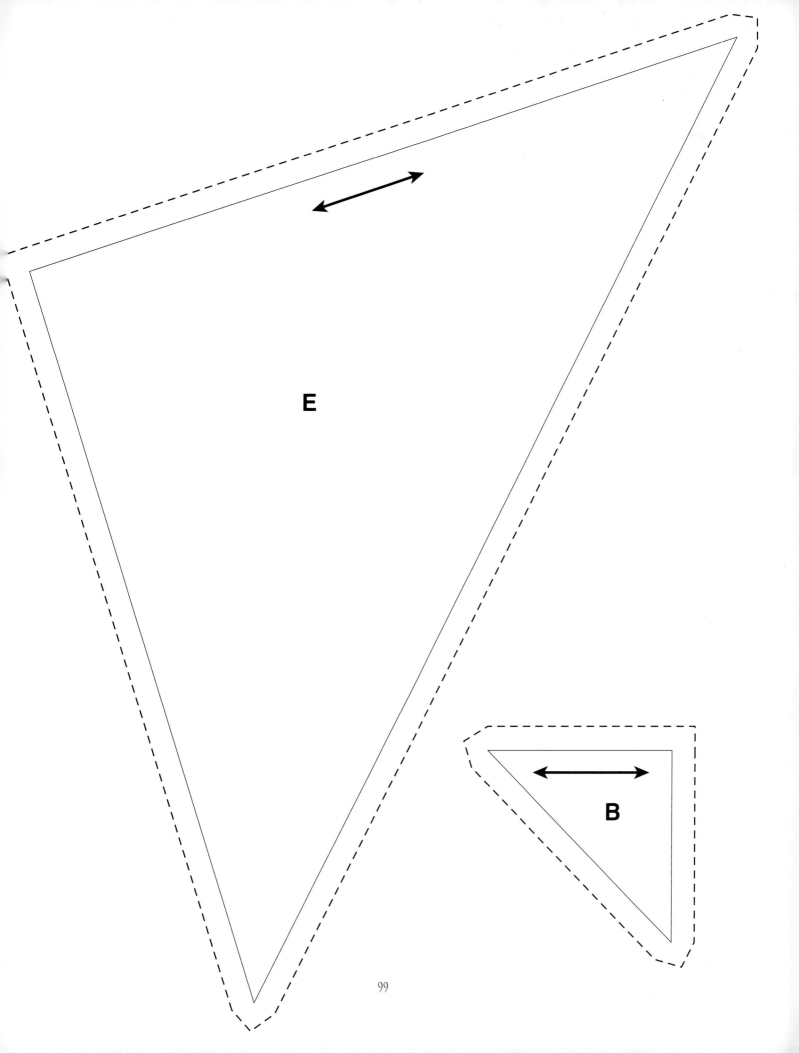

E

B

Basket of Star Flowers appliquéd by Susie Kepley, Lee's Summit, Missouri.

BASKET OF STAR FLOWERS

Original Design by Edie McGinnis
12" finished block

Fabric needed: background, medium (flowers), striped (basket fabric), green (leaves) and black (flower centers).

From the background fabric, cut one 13" square.

Use your favorite method of appliqué and remember to add 1/4" if you are appliquéing by hand.

From the medium fabric, cut three flowers using templates D, E and F, one bud using template G and one partial flower using template H.

From the green fabric, cut one 1" x 20-3/4" bias strip, two leaves using template J and one calyx using template I.

From the black fabric, cut circles using templates A, B and C.

From the striped fabric, cut one piece using template K, one bias strip 1-1/2" x 18" and one 2" x 7-3/4" bias strip.

Fold the background 13" square in quarters and finger press a crease along each fold line for placement purposes. Then mark the position of the handle, basket bottom, flowers and leaves

Millions of brilliantly colored glass beads of every size and shape were also found aboard the Arabia. The beads were also intended as trade goods. Seed beads made up the majority found but there were also larger ones to beautify the Native American's clothing or to string as a lovely necklace.

using the position chart on page 103.

Fold the dark bias strips in 1/4" on each side and press.

Pin the bias strip for the handle in place and appliqué onto the background square.

Fold the green bias strip in 1/4" on each side and press.

Trim the green bias strip into stems measuring 5-3/4", 5-1/4", 4", 3" and 2" lengths. Pin and appliqué the strips in place.

Position, pin and appliqué the leaves next.

Now appliqué the bottom of the basket in place. Sew the bias strip in place after turning under 1/4" on both sides of the strip.

Add the bud, flowers and the centers of the flowers.

Trim the background square to 12-1/2" to complete the block.

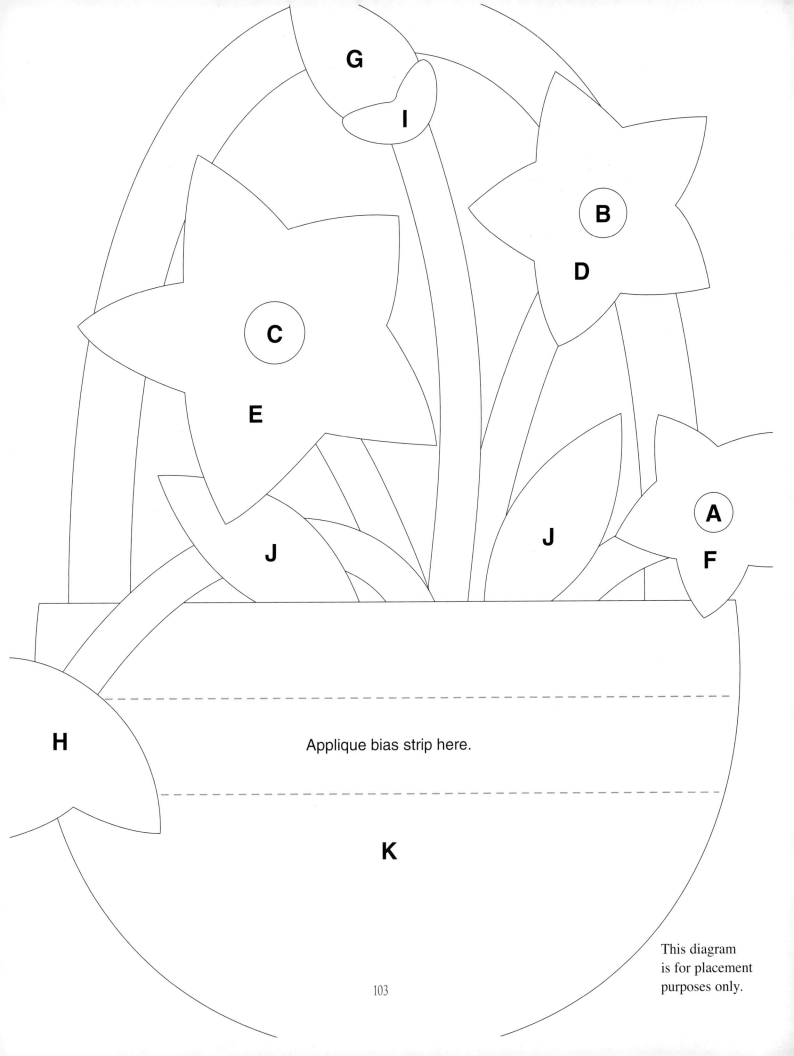

G

I

B

D

C

E

A

F

J

J

H

Applique bias strip here.

K

103

This diagram
is for placement
purposes only.

C

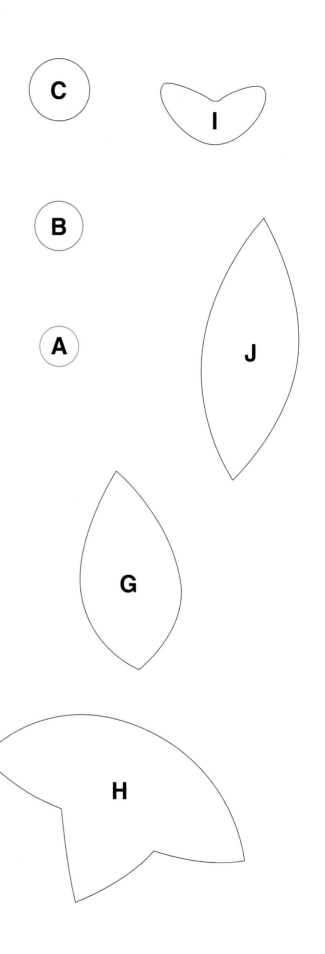

B

A

F

104

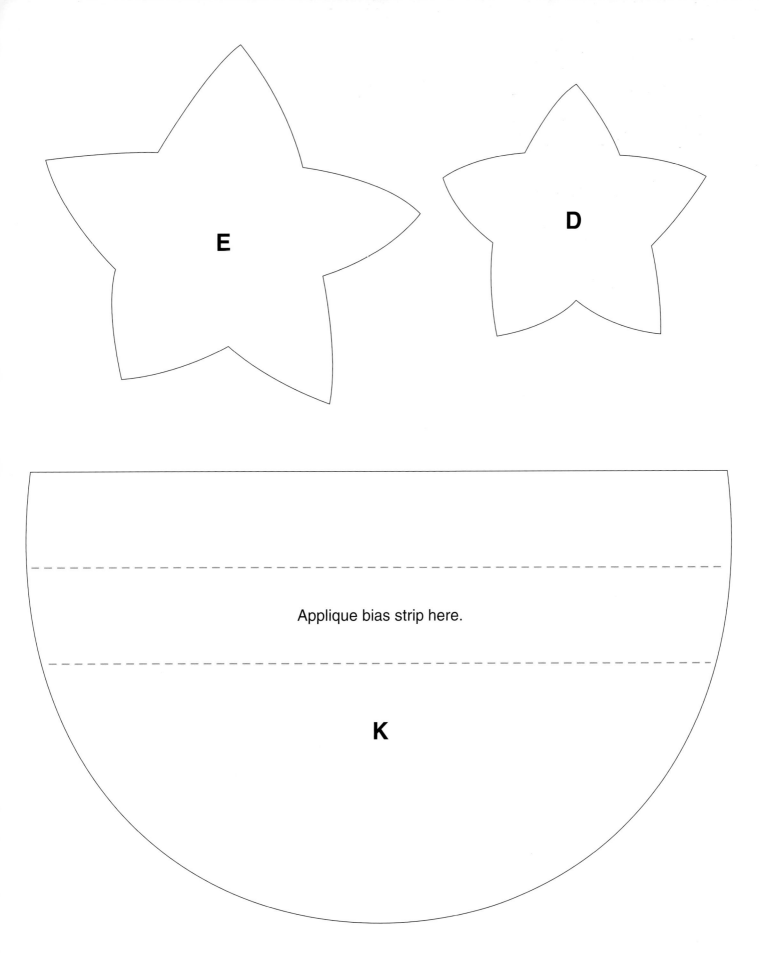

E

D

Applique bias strip here.

K

Flowers in a Basket pieced by Linda Kriesel, Independence, Missouri.

FLOWERS IN A BASKET

August 20, 1941
12" finished block

Fabric needed: background, medium and dark.

From the background fabric, cut 2 triangles using template B, one scant 4-1/2" square (template A), two 3" x 10-1/8" rectangles (template C).

From the medium fabric, cut eight diamonds using template E.

From the dark fabric, cut eight diamonds using template E, one triangle using template F and one 3" square (template D).

Sew a medium E diamond to a dark E diamond.

Then sew a dark E diamond to a medium E diamond.

Not only did the ladies living through the hardships of life on the frontier need flowers to brighten their lives, they also needed the same luxuries to brighten their days as we modern women. Bound for the frontier stores on the Arabia's ports of call were 23 bottles of perfume, 18 bottles of coconut-scented lotion, 32 bottles of unscented lotion and 24 ironstone pots, 42 hand held mirrors and 11 glass jars of cosmetics. Then there were the necessities: toothbrushes, hairbrushes, eyeglasses, combs and around 6,000 steel hairpins.

When visiting the museum, one can take a sniff of the different perfumes discovered. The Hawleys sent samples of both to France and had them duplicated. Bottles of the delightful scents can be purchased in the gift shop.

Sew the two rows together to make a large E diamond. Make four of these large diamonds.

Stitch a background B triangle to the top part of a large E diamond as shown.

Now add another large diamond.

Next add the background A square.

Then add the third large diamond.

Add the remaining B triangle next.

Now sew on the last E diamond.

Next sew on the dark F piece to the base of the basket.

Add a background C strip to one side of the
basket.

Sew the dark D square to a background
C strip.

Sew on the strip to complete the block.

Now sew a dark B triangle to one side of a background C triangle and a medium B triangle to the other side of the triangle as shown making a flying geese unit.

Do the same with the other background C triangle except change the position of the medium and dark triangles.

Sew the two remaining dark B triangles to the two D background strips.

Next sew the background and a dark E triangle together.

To construct the block, sew the background A square to a medium/background half-square triangle unit.

Add the flying geese unit next to complete the row.

Sew four half-square triangle units together as shown ending with a dark/background unit.

Sew this row to row one.

Next sew a background/medium half-square triangle unit to a dark/light half-square triangle.

To the left of these two units, sew the remaining flying geese unit and to the right add the dark/background large E half-square triangle unit. This makes two rows combined and should now look like this.

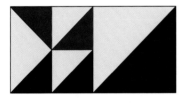

Sew this to the two previous rows you made. At this point your block should look like this.

Now add the two D strips to which the two dark B triangles were attached.

Complete the block by sewing on the remaining background E triangle.

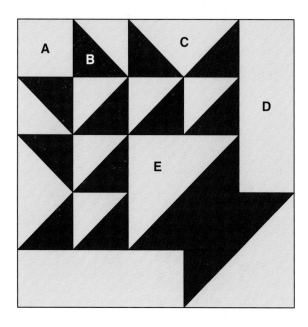

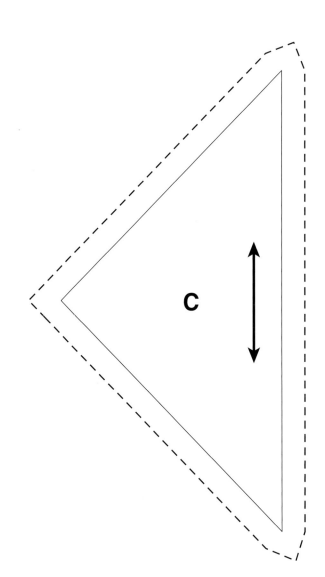

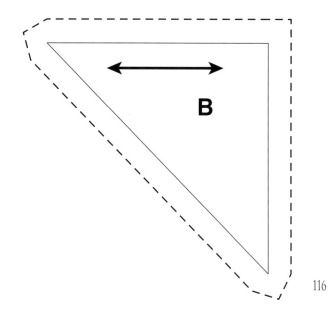

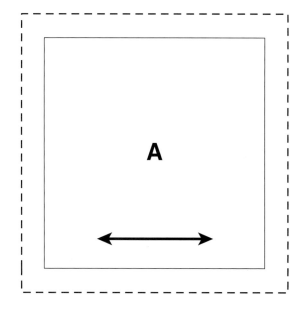

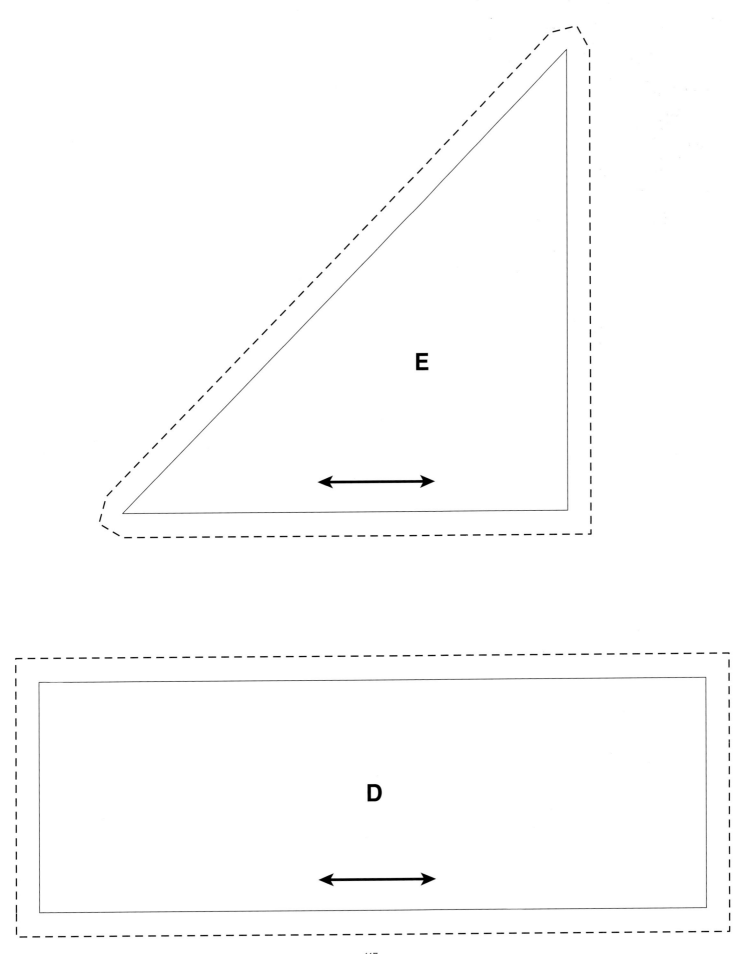

E

D

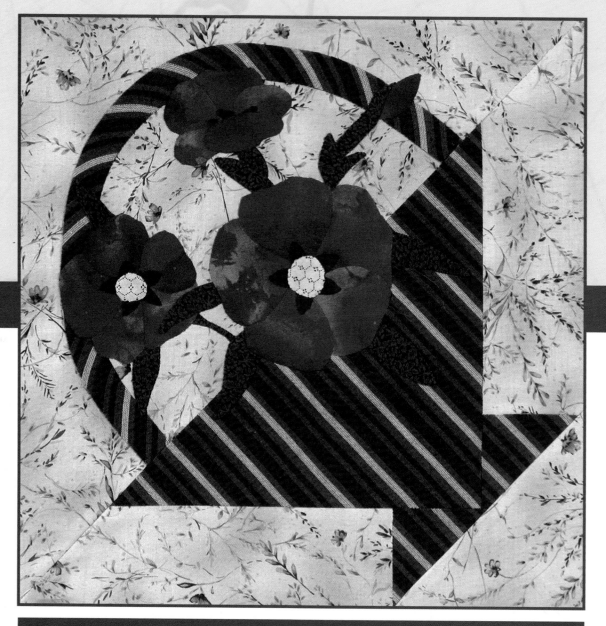

Posey's Basket appliquéd and pieced by Margaret Falen, Grain Valley, Missouri.

POSEY'S BASKET

Original Design by Edie McGinnis
12" finished block

Fabric needed: background (may be light or dark), green, yellow, light purple, dark purple and one stripe.

From the background fabric, cut one 12-7/8" triangle (no template given), one 4-7/8" triangle (template D) and two 8-1/2" strips (template B and Br).

From the striped fabric, cut one 8-7/8" triangle (template A), two 2-7/8" triangles (template C) and one 1-1/2" x 18" bias strip. To line up the stripes, place template A on the fabric so the arrow runs with the straight of grain. This will position the stripes properly. Do the same with the template C triangles.

Authors Note: When hand appliquéing, add 1/8" - 1/4" seam allowance to each appliqué piece.

From the light purple, cut the flower petals. They are templates one through five for the large flower, 1a through 5a for the medium flower and 1b through 5b for the small flower. Also, you will need to cut one bud.

From the dark purple, cut 5 ovals using template 1-1, 5 ovals using template 2-2 and 3 ovals using template 3-3.

This basket of rock roses is named in honor of my father, Mel Renner. My dad worked at a distillery in Pekin, Illinois, as a cooper. In short, he made and repaired barrels. My grandfather, Leonard Renner, was also a cooper. Both of the men worked together and for some odd reason, carried the nicknames Posey and Little Posey. When my grandfather died, my dad became Posey. Both my grandfather and my dad could have fit right in and earned a living in 1856. Aboard the Arabia were tools used in the cooper's trade such as draw knives, mallets and barrel lifting tongs.

From the green fabric, cut leaves using templates 1L through 9L.

From the yellow fabric, cut two circles using templates E1 and E2.

Using the placement guide on page 123, lightly mark the position of the basket handle, flowers and leaves on the 12-7/8" background triangle.

Sew the B and Br pieces to the striped C triangles.

Sew the pieces to the sides of the 8-7/8" striped triangle (template C) as shown.

Add the background D triangle.

Appliqué the basket handle in place.

Sew the top of the basket to the base.

Pin all of the appliqué pieces in place. Stitch all the pieces in place using your favorite method of appliqué. Embroider the stem from the medium-sized flower to finish the block.

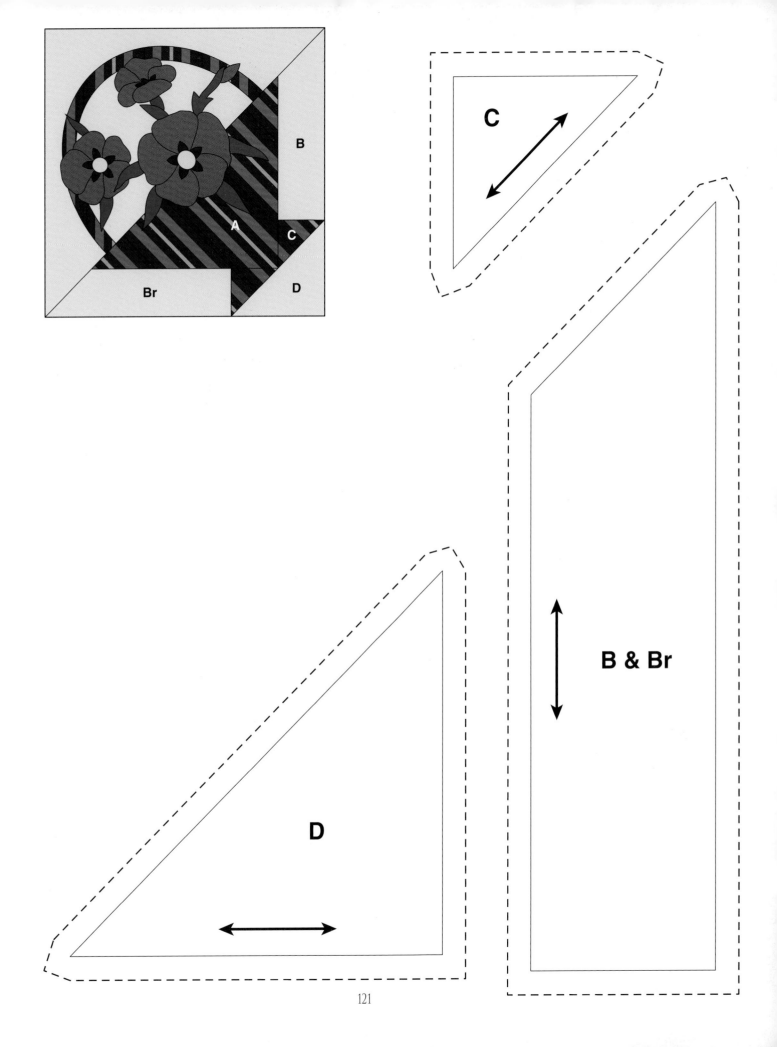

C

B & Br

D

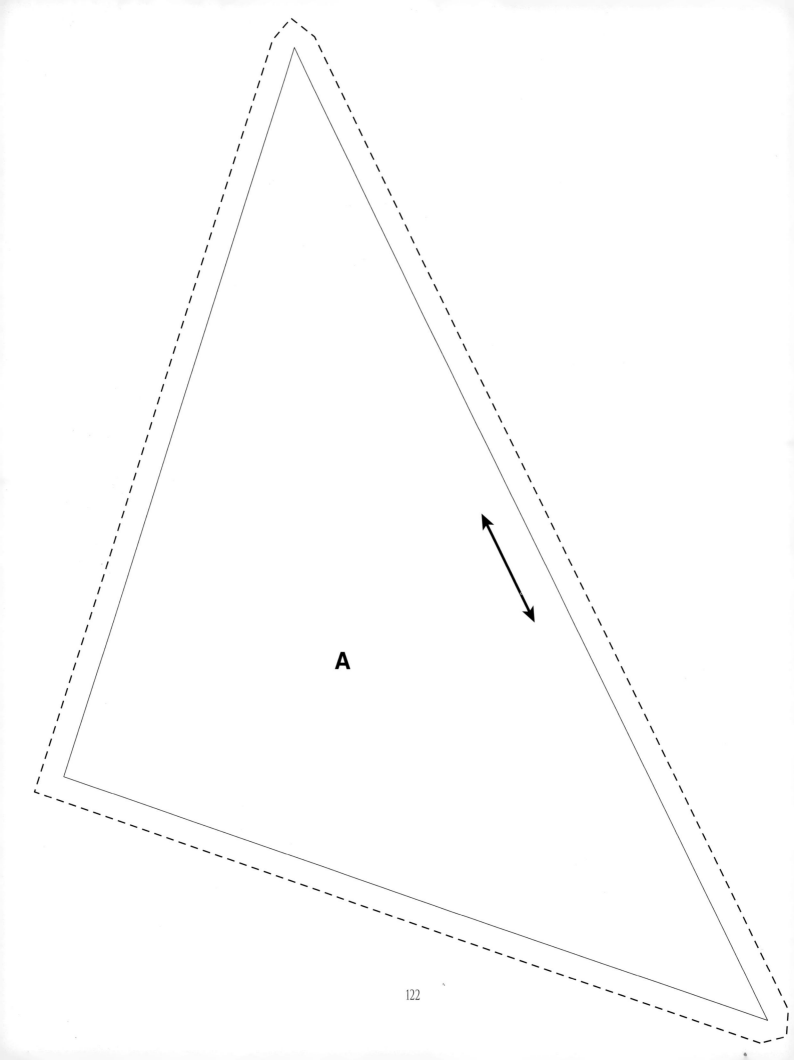

A

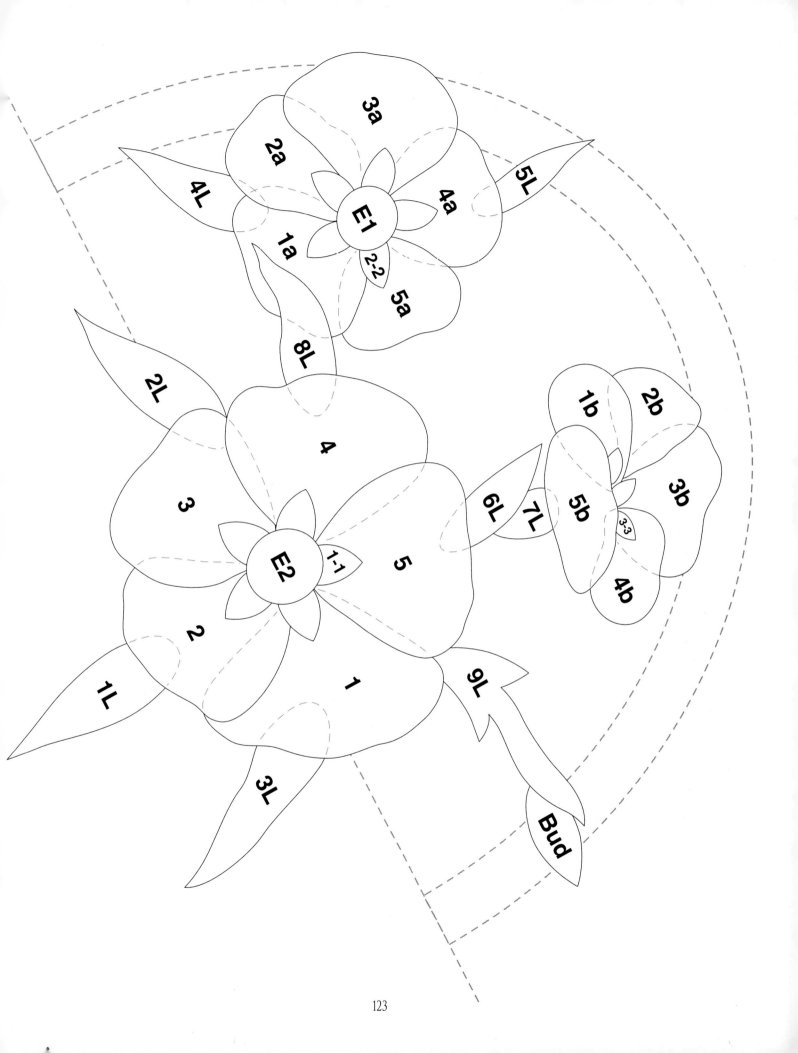

123

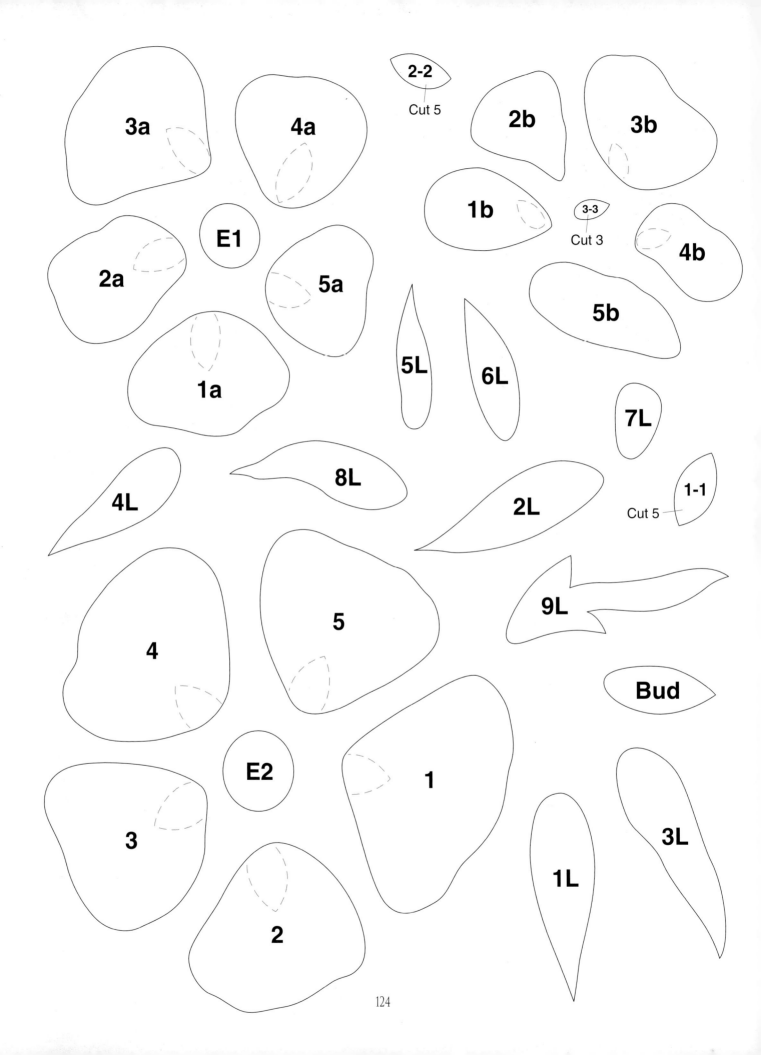

3a

4a

2-2
Cut 5

2b

3b

E1

2a

1b

3-3
Cut 3

4b

5a

5b

1a

5L

6L

7L

4L

8L

2L

1-1
Cut 5

4

5

9L

Bud

E2

1

3

3L

1L

2

124

Judy Streu, Liberty, Missouri, shares this indigo and white basket quilt from her collection. The basket is a variation of the Basket of Oranges pattern in which the appliqué was not added.

Shari's Basket pieced by Shari McMillan, Marquette Heights, Illinois.

SHARI'S BASKET

Original Design by Shari McMillan
Marquette Heights, Illinois
12" finished block

Fabric needed: light and dark.

From the light fabric, cut two 2-1/2" x 8-1/2" strips (template B), one 4-7/8" triangle (template C), one 6-7/8" triangle (template D) and ten 2-7/8" squares or 19 triangles using template A.

From the dark fabric, cut one piece using template E and eleven 2-7/8" squares or 21 triangles using template A.

Following the directions in the front of the book, make 18 half-square triangle units. You will have one light square and two dark squares left over. Cut the squares from corner to corner on the diagonal to make triangles. After constructing the block, you will have one light and one dark triangle left over.

To make the block, begin by sewing three half-square triangle units together. Attach these to the D triangle.

Thanks to my sister, Shari, for this pattern. She is the kind of woman who can learn to do anything she likes. She has taught herself to make bobbin lace, tat, knit, crochet and quilt. Had she lived in 1856 and been waiting for the packet Arabia to stock her local store, she would have been delighted to find bobbins for her lace making, etuis for needles, skeins of wool yarn, embroidery floss made from silk, silk thread and wool rickrack and bias tape.

Now sew four half-square triangle units together as shown. Sew this row to the left side of the D triangle.

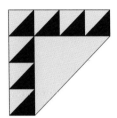

Next sew a dark A triangle to two half-square triangle units.

Then sew a dark A triangle to one half-square triangle unit.

Sew the two rows together and add a dark triangle to the top as shown.

Sew this unit to the D triangle.

Now sew four half-square triangles together in a vertical row and add a B strip.

Sew this to the right side of the block.

Next sew the light A triangle to the dark E piece. Add the light C triangle to make a square.

Sew the remaining four half-square triangles together in a horizontal row. Add the remaining B strip.

Then add on the AEC square.

Sew the strip on to complete the block.

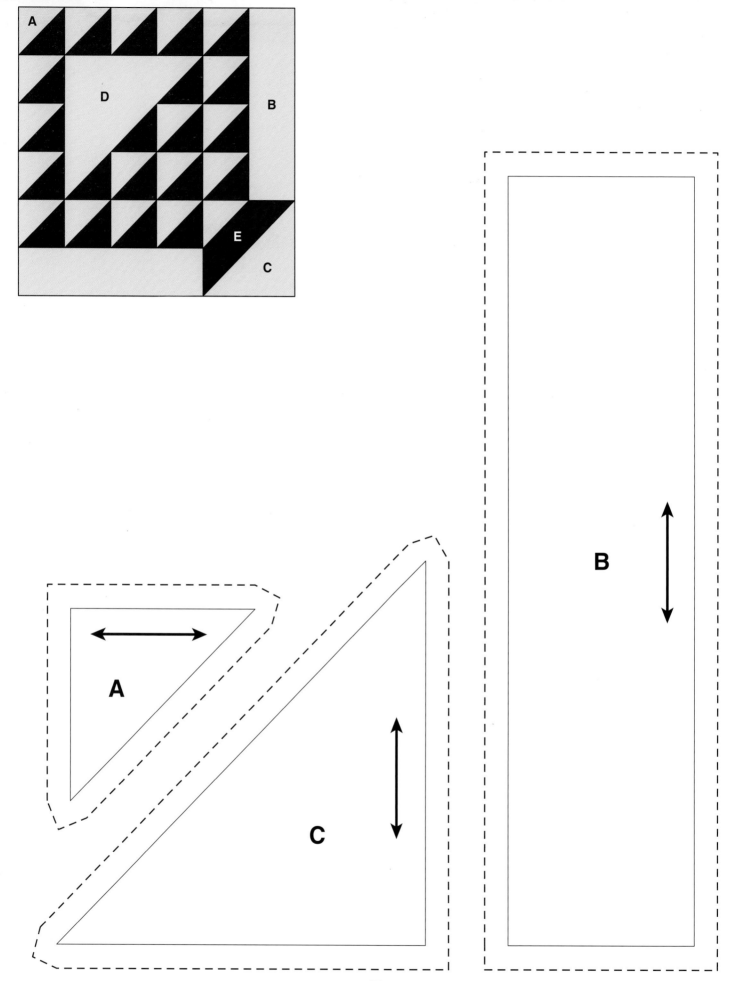

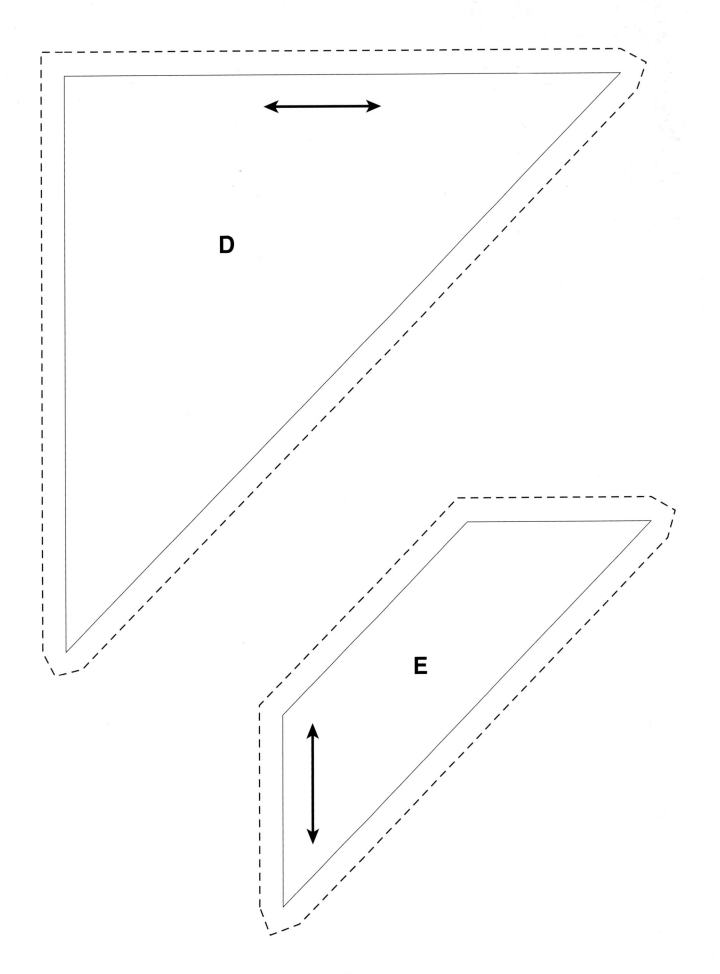

Basket of Diamonds pieced by Linda Kriesel, Independence, Missouri.

BASKET OF DIAMONDS

August 18, 1937
12" finished block

Fabric needed: background, medium and dark.

From the background fabric, cut one piece using template A, one piece using template Ar, one piece using template B and one piece using template Br. and one triangle using template C.

From the medium fabric, cut four diamonds using template E and two triangles using template D.

From the dark fabric, cut four diamonds using template E and one triangle using template C.

Sew a dark E diamond to a medium E diamond. Make four of these units.

Sew two of the units together as shown.

Perhaps no diamonds were found aboard the steamboat but thirteen pairs of gold-plated earrings were found as well as 41 brooches, 10 gold-plated rings and 6 gold rings. I found it fascinating that some of the earrings were made for pierced ears.

Sew the other two units to either side of the lower part of the large diamond as shown.

Sew the medium D and Dr triangles onto the dark C triangle.

Sew this to the bottom of the diamond basket.

Add the B and Br pieces.

Sew the background A piece onto the right top portion of the large diamond and the background Ar piece onto the left top portion to complete the block.

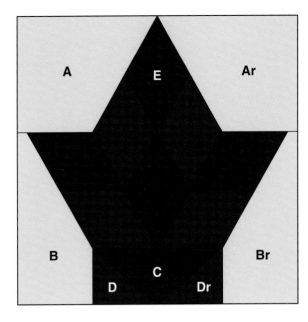

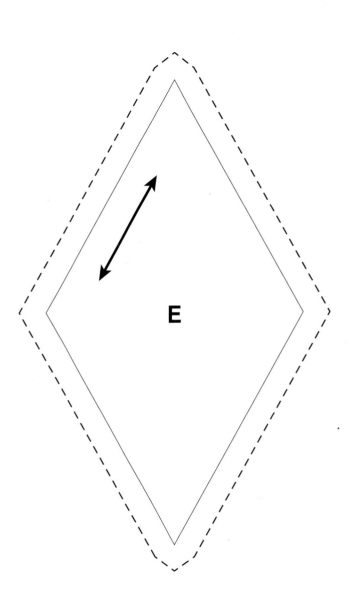

E

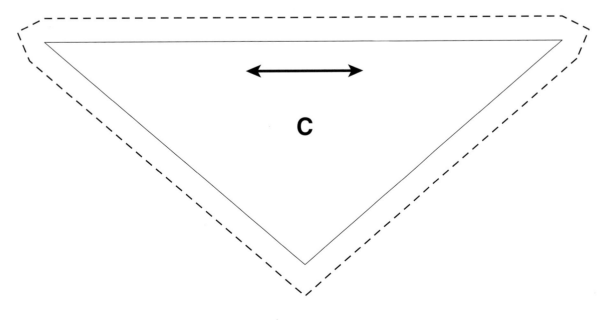

C

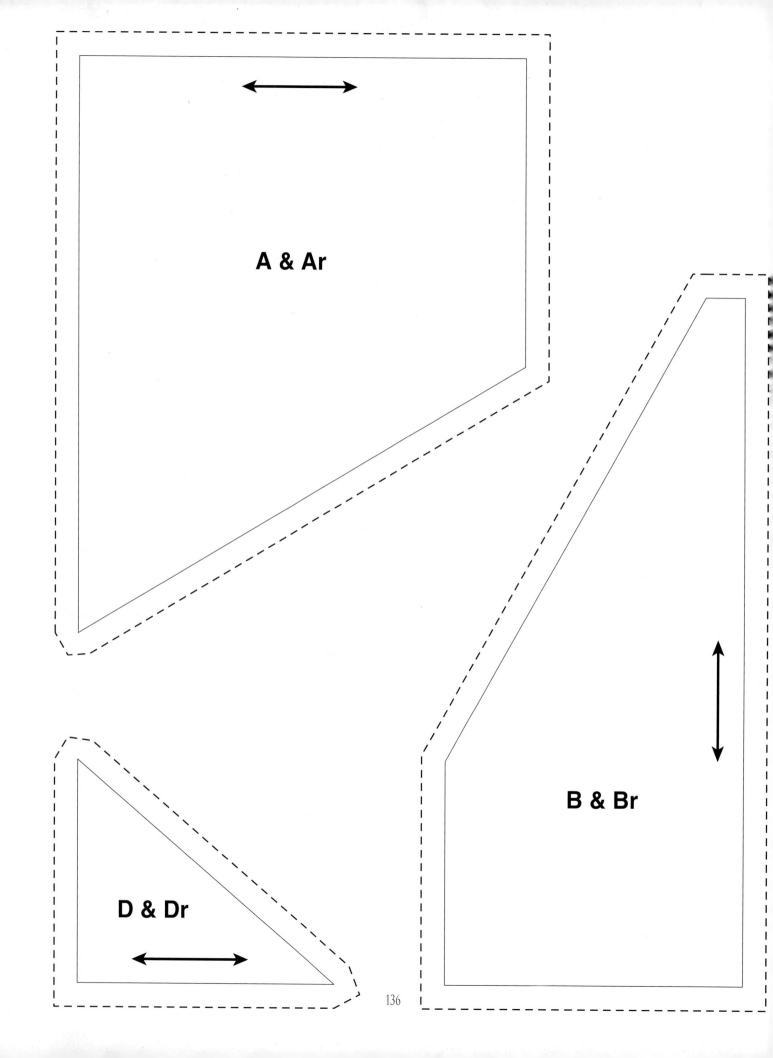

A & Ar

B & Br

D & Dr

Judy Hill of Independence, Missouri, owns this example of the Orange Basket quilt pattern sans oranges. Judy's eighty-two year old mother made this quilt for her.

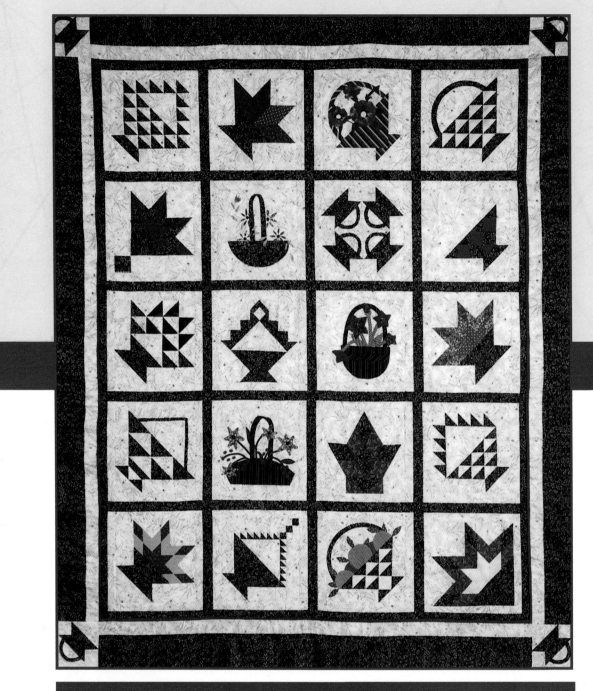

Baskets of Treasures Quilt

PUTTING IT ALL TOGETHER

It's time to end our tour of the Arabia Steamboat Museum. The pitiful part of this is that you've not seen it all. You've barely had a peek at all the wonders this museum holds. Out of over 200 tons of cargo, you only got to learn about 20 items. You haven't even met Lawrence. I know you must hunger for more. Of course there is only one thing a person can do about that. Come to Kansas City and see the Arabia Steamboat Museum in person. It will be the highlight of your day.

While you are waiting for your plans to gel, let's put our quilt together.

We made one May Basket for each corner of the quilt. We set the baskets aside until we were ready to put the outside borders on the quilt.

We began with 20 blocks. We put four blocks in each row across and had five rows going down. We sewed a 1-3/4" strip of background fabric all around each 12-1/2" unfinished block. Each block was then squared to 15".

After we finished squaring each block, we cut 2" strips for sashing. On this quilt we used the black fabric, which was our dark color, for sashing strips. We sewed the strips to the blocks so they would be on the inner part of each square. We then measured the quilt across the center and across the top and bottom to get our measurement for the sashing we would need for the top and bottom of the quilt. Then we measured through the center of the quilt and along the two long sides to get the length of the strips we would need for the side sashing.

We cut two of our strips 2" wide by the width of the quilt and two of our strips 2" wide by the length of the quilt. We had to piece the strips together to make them the right measurement. We then added the strips to the edges.

We then cut 1" burgundy strips across the width of the fabric. After piecing the strips together to get the correct width and length of the top, the strips were folded and pressed, then sewn onto the black border and pressed again so it would lie flat against the quilt. We used

1/2 yard for these strips.

Again we measured the quilt through the center and across each end to determine the width of the quilt. This number gives the width of the borders one needs to put on the quilt. We also measured through the center and down each side to determine the length of the borders needed on each side.

We then cut strips 2-1/2" wide of background fabric. We sewed enough strips together to make four borders long enough to go on the top, the bottom and on each side of the quilt. We cut strips of our dark fabric 4-1/2" wide to go around the quilt also. We sewed the dark and background strips together for the sides and the tops.

After cutting our strips the correct measurement, we sewed the top and bottom

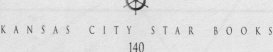

borders to the quilt. We then sewed the 6" baskets to the side borders and added these to the quilt.

Our quilt measured 82" wide by 101" long.

Fabric requirements: (Measurements are approximate and generous.)

Background: 3-1/2 yards

Dark: 4 yards (includes binding fabric)

Burgundy: 7 fat eighths and 1/2 yard for the inside border strip.

Green: fat eighths of 4 different greens.

Striped fabrics for baskets: 2 different stripes, 1 fat quarter for each.

Dark Orange Plaids: 2 fat eighths or scraps for Basket of Oranges block.

Tan Plaid: 1 fat eighth or scraps.

Light Tan: 1/2 yard.

One of the things I like best about quilting is the opportunity to make everything personal. I enjoy choosing my fabric and watching everything come together just the way I imagined it would.

If you choose to make this quilt, I hope you make it your own way and add your own personal touch. Embellish if you like. Make red baskets or blue baskets or purple baskets. Use all the patterns or only one. Buy fabric or use up your scraps. Make the most of what you have in your stash.

Quilt store owners can seldom reorder fabric. So, even though the fabric in this quilt is relatively current, you may not be able to find it. Don't let this bother you. Instead of duplicating the fabric, choose instead to duplicate the value. Trust me, your quilt will be gorgeous.

Judy Streu, Liberty, Missouri, owns this pillow made from the Grape Basket pattern.

Small May Baskets adorn the corners of a wall quilt made by Shari McMillan, Marquette Heights, Illinois. The hand pieced and hand quilted wall quilt features a cherry basket in the center set on point and has a May Basket in each corner.

References

Last Days on the Water, article by Tim Janicke, *Star magazine -
The Kansas City Star*, February 18, 2001.

The People Who Saved the Arabia, by Jill Silva, *The Kansas City
Star*, Style Section - March 28, 1992.

Treasure in a Cornfield, by Greg Hawley, Paddlewheel Press, 1998.

www.1856.com - Website of **The Arabia Steamboat Museum**.

Notes from a tour of **The Arabia Steamboat Museum**.

ABOUT THE AUTHOR

Edie McGinnis has been quilting for almost 30 years. She is a member of the American Quilter's Society and the Quilters Guild of Greater Kansas City. This is the sixth quilt book she has written about *The Kansas City Star* quilt patterns. She teaches quilting classes and gives lectures about *The Star* quilt patterns.